Kate wakes up in her kitchen, having no idea where she had been for five hours. The only clue she has is a note she left for herself on her desk, stating that she was going to see someone named Naomi.

With some investigation, she discovers Naomi is a therapist she has been seeing for months to discuss her blackouts and dissociation. However, she hasn't been attending the sessions as Kate, but under a different name: Veronica.

Once she realizes she is experiencing dissociation, Kate takes a deep dive into her life, trying to uncover her alters and make peace with the people she shares a headspace with.

As she unlocks secrets hidden even from herself, she has the support of her best friend, Brielle, and her therapist, but not everyone is out to help her.

MISSING

CHELSI ROBICHAUD

A NineStar Press Publication
www.ninestarpress.com

Missing

© 2025 Chelsi Robichaud
Cover Art © 2025 Melody Pond

This is a work of fiction. Names, characters, places, and incidents are either the product of the author's imagination or are used fictitiously. Any resemblance to actual persons living or dead, business establishments, events, or locales is entirely coincidental.

All rights reserved. No part of this publication may be reproduced in any material form, whether by printing, photocopying, scanning or otherwise without the written permission of the publisher. To request permission and all other inquiries, contact NineStar Press at Contact@ninestarpress.com.

First Edition, April 2025

ISBN: 978-1-64890-865-1

Also available in eBook, ISBN: 978-1-64890-864-4

CONTENT WARNING:

This book contains references to the physical and emotional abuse of a child by a parent, self-harm (past occurrence), and depictions of therapy sessions, which are not prescriptive and may not reflect real experiences in clinical settings.

I would like to dedicate this book to Jade and Stephane. Thank you so much for your support.

Chapter One

October 2022

Sheets of rain poured down from the sky. I moved through the crowds of people. The raindrops hit the ground rhythmically like drums, drowning out the sound of footsteps.

I sighed in relief as I made it to the shelter of my home. Nobody greeted me on the road. Everyone was probably inside, where it was warm. I was unfazed by the cold.

When I got inside, I found a clear patch of floor near the kitchen and lay down. I wasn't sure how long I lay there. I didn't even check the time when I came in.

"What's going on with you?" Mike asked in horror when he walked through the door.

I was curled up on the floor, my hair and clothes completely soaked from the rain. I shook my head. "I don't know."

"You're sitting on the floor. Come on, honey, get up." He

helped me stand. "What were you thinking, lying down on the floor? Why didn't you get changed?"

"I don't know."

"Where have you been?"

I bit my lip, hard enough to draw blood. I didn't want to say "I don't know" a third time, but I really had no explanation for why I was where I was.

Mike guided me to the couch. He fetched a towel and put it down so I wouldn't soak the furniture. "Here, sit down." I sat. "What's the last thing you remember?"

"I remember walking to the apartment," I said. "I remember it raining."

"And before that?"

"Not much." I looked down at my fingers, pruned from the dampness. "I must've been out for hours."

"The last time you texted me was at 2:00," he said. "It's 7:00 now."

Five hours. I had five hours unaccounted for. My head spun. How could I have just forgotten what I was up to for *five hours*?

Mike must have sensed my impending panic. He pressed his hands to either side of my shoulders. "We'll figure this out."

I took out my phone. Mike had tried calling me during the time I had been out. "Missing" almost felt more appropriate—although at this point it seemed I had been missing even to myself. I scanned my text messages to see if there were any conversations I had opened while I was out. Nothing. I hadn't talked to anyone—I had just disappeared, and my memories went with me.

"Do you think we could retrace your steps?" he asked. "The last thing you told me was that you were going to do groceries today. By the looks of the kitchen, though, you didn't get to it."

"Guess not," I muttered. I was entirely depleted of energy. I wanted to sleep, but the anxiety of not knowing where I was for most of the day kept me awake.

"Let's get you out of these wet clothes and into something warmer, okay?"

I got up from the couch and followed Mike into the bedroom. I stripped off my wet clothes. He took them and tossed them into the dryer. I picked out a comfortable pair of sweatpants and a plain black T-shirt.

I noticed a note sitting on my bedroom desk. It was written in a hand I didn't recognize. The desk had been tidied, too. I must have cleaned it before I left. The note read: *Going out to see Naomi. Be back before dark.*

I sat down at the desk and read the note again. I didn't have any friends named Naomi. But it only made sense that I had written this note before I blacked out.

I picked up my phone and searched through my contacts. Naomi. I found her. Her area code was local. Which meant I really *had* gone out to meet with her.

"Babe," I called.

Mike shot into the room. "What's up? You need a doctor?"

"I don't know yet," I said. "Look at this note."

He stood behind me and read over my shoulder. "Who's Naomi?"

"That's what I'm trying to figure out." I showed him my phone. "She's in my contacts. But I have no idea who she is."

Mike pressed a hand to his chin. He paused for a few moments, thinking. "Should we...call her?"

"I can at least text her," I said.

Me: *Hi. This is Kate.*

Naomi: *You left in a hurry. Everything OK?*

"So, you were with her," he said. "This is great. Maybe she can tell us why you were out for so long."

How could I have been out with a new friend all day and not remember a thing? It didn't make any sense.

> **Me:** *I don't remember meeting you. How did we get in touch?*

I watched as Naomi typed, then stopped. Eventually, my phone chimed as a text came through.

> **Naomi:** *I think you need to tell Mike about your dissociation.*

> **Me:** *Is that what you call the blackout? Were you with me when it happened?*

> **Naomi:** *Go check your desk drawer for the journal. It might help.*

I pushed back my desk chair to get to the drawer. When I pulled it open, I spotted the journal right away. It was black and green, with a Celtic knot on the cover.

"I remember buying this journal online, but I haven't filled it out yet," I said. "I bought it to write music in."

"Let's see." I could hear a note of fear in Mike's tone.

I opened the journal. A page had been filled.

"I don't remember writing this." But even as I said it, I knew there was no other possibility. It was my handwriting. I checked the most recent entry. It was from the beginning of the week.

> *October 17th, 2022*
>
> *Things are getting worse. Hard to handle. I'm not sure*

when I should tell Mike about this—Veronica thinks it's best he stays out of it. She always had an issue with him, though. Thinks that he can't be trusted. I don't know why she feels this way. It might be a trauma reaction. Jer thinks that he'll be receptive to it all. I have no way of knowing. I'm thinking of going to visit Naomi to talk it all out. She's always been supportive.

The sound of clothes tumbling in the dryer was all that could be heard. I let out my breath with a deep exhale. Mike's brows were knit together in concern.

"You don't remember writing any of this?" he asked.

"Not a word."

"Who's Veronica? And Jer?"

"I have no idea." I pressed a hand to my forehead. My head was pounding. I felt like memories were dancing on the edge of my conscious mind, but they were too far out of my reach to fully understand. "The names mean something to me, but I don't know what."

Mike crossed his arms in front of his chest. "Why would one of your friends think I shouldn't be trusted? We've been together for months now. I don't think I've done anything to warrant that."

"Me neither," I said, and meant it. Things had been good between Mike and me ever since we'd started dating.

Mike took the journal from me and closed it. "Let's explore this more tomorrow, okay? I think you need some rest. I'm sure you'll remember everything once you've slept a bit."

I wished I shared his certainty. It wasn't like I had forgotten to pick up the milk at the store—I had forgotten almost an entire day, and there were now three people in my life who apparently knew far more about me than I knew about them.

"How can I sleep right now knowing I've essentially been

leading a double life?" I asked. "None of this makes sense, and I don't recognize any of those people. I don't even know who Naomi is. What if they're dangerous?"

"I don't think you'd make friends with dangerous people." Mike did his best to comfort me.

"But if neither of us know, then how can we be sure?"

He hugged me. "I don't know, babe. I don't know. But we'll figure it out together, okay? I just don't want you to overwhelm yourself. Not when I just found you on the floor."

I checked my phone one final time before heading to bed.

Naomi: *Tell Kate everything will be OK.*

I wondered who she was, and how exactly she knew that.

*

I slept deeply. When I woke up, I checked to see if I had dreamed it all. But no—the journal sat on the desk where I had left it.

It was Saturday. Mike had stayed the night and lay snoring in my bed. I appreciated his concern for me. I had told him he didn't need to stay, but the man was terrified, I could see it written plainly on his face. He wouldn't rest easy if he went home.

I made myself a pot of coffee. When it was done, I poured myself a cup and beelined for my desk. I read the entry dated October 17th again. I mentioned two people other than Naomi in the entry. If I had her in my phone as a contact, wouldn't I have Veronica and Jer as well? I took out my phone and scrolled through my contacts. They weren't there. I looked for variations on their names. Nothing. I recognized every contact in my phone except for Naomi.

I peeked over at Mike. He was still fast asleep. I hurried to the bathroom and checked my face. I looked tired. I applied some cream to my eyes, then some makeup to my face. I appeared a little less tired, but there was something...*wrong* about the way I looked. My eyes weren't quite the right shade. The cut of my cheek seemed wrong—like the shadows were falling incorrectly. I pressed my fingertips to my face. It seemed too narrow, not recognizable as mine.

I left the bathroom and took out my clothes I had forgotten in the dryer the day before. I had been wearing a pale-blue dress with flowers on it. A dress that was meant more for the summer than for fall. I would have had to dig this outfit out of the clothes I had packed up and put away. And my hair—I recalled dimly that before the rain hit, I had curled it. I usually left it straight, preferring not to use heat tools. But I could see the hair curler I had left out, resting on the bathroom counter.

My only lead toward finding more information was Naomi. I had her contact information, but not much else. Where did she live? How far would I have to travel to get to her? Knots formed in my stomach as I realized I probably already had traveled to see her the day before—and got stuck in the rain on my way home.

"Kate?" Mike said groggily.

"Hey." I walked over to the bed. "How'd you sleep?"

"Fine, thanks." He rubbed his eyes. "What about you? Did you remember anything?"

"No. Nothing. I was hoping to go find that Naomi person today. Maybe ask her a few questions."

"I'll come," he said, swinging his legs out of the bed. He grabbed his jeans from off the floor.

"You don't have to," I told him. "You've already done enough. Basically babysitting me all night. I'm doing better today."

"But you still haven't seen a doctor," he shot back. "And we don't know if it'll happen again."

"I don't think I need to see a doctor yet. It's only happened once. I can go on my own."

"You *can*, but you shouldn't." He put on his shirt. "Let me come with you. If something bad happens, at least you won't be alone."

"All right." I sighed and sat on the bed. "None of this makes sense. I checked my phone to see if either of the people I mentioned in my journal were contacts. Nope."

Mike picked up his keys from my bedside table. "Ask Naomi where she lives."

I pulled out my phone and asked Naomi for her address. She responded within seconds. Once we had her address, we headed out the door.

*

Naomi's place was a duplex nestled in an affluent-looking neighborhood. The houses were well-kept and so were all the gardens. People clearly had time and resources to pool into their appearances here, and so did she. Her house was white with a large black door. It looked like it had been freshly painted.

"Seems you have a rich friend," Mike said as we walked up her driveway.

"Seems so."

I rang the doorbell. A woman with brown, bouncing curls opened the door. She smiled widely when she saw me. She wore a white blouse with black dress pants.

"Kate!" she exclaimed, motioning for me to enter. "Please, come on in. And you must be Mike."

"Hi," he said.

We both entered her house. The first thing I noticed was the wide array of plants. There were some hanging from the ceiling, while others were positioned close to the window. A few small ones even stood on shelves next to the door. The rest of the decor had a modern feel, with exposed wood on the walls.

"You must have so many questions," Naomi said. "Let's sit down. I made us some tea."

We followed her to the living room. Her couches were all black leather. The coffee table was made from oak, and coasters were neatly placed in front of our seats. She had prepared for our arrival. I watched her rush from the living room to the kitchen to fetch a pot of tea, a nervous crease around her eyes. The way she raced about her home made me wonder if our abrupt visit was unwelcome.

She poured us both a steaming hot cup of tea. "I didn't expect to see you again so soon."

I laughed nervously. "I didn't expect to be…back. Here, I mean. In this house."

"Kate is having trouble remembering what brought her here yesterday," Mike said. "We were hoping you could help us out."

How did I tell this woman I didn't even remember who she was? Her face seemed familiar, like someone I had seen on television once, or in a dream. Not a person I had actually ever met.

"Kate wasn't here yesterday," Naomi said, sitting down in front of us. "Not exactly."

"But she was with you?" Mike asked. "You said she left in a hurry."

"She was." Naomi had a funny expression as she looked at me. I couldn't decipher it at all. It seemed to be a mix of concern, hesitation, and a faint hint of amusement. "But Kate wasn't here."

"You keep saying that," I said. "If I wasn't here, then where was I?"

"It was your alters who were here with me."

"My what?"

Naomi folded her hands in her lap. "We knew this day would come soon. Where you'd be conscious of your actions. Like we discussed, it's impossible for you to hide it forever..."

"Hide what?" I asked. "I'm sorry, but I'm not following."

"You were experiencing dissociation yesterday," Naomi said. "I was helping you through it."

"And you're...what? A doctor?" Mike asked.

"I'm a counseling student," Naomi said. "I've been helping...Kate out with her dissociation for the last few weeks."

"Weeks?" I repeated, dumbfounded. "You mean I've been coming here for weeks and just forgetting it all?"

"You don't forget it, not really," she replied. "You remember our sessions enough to journal about them and come back to discuss them."

"What qualifies you to be working with her?" Mike asked. "No offense, but you're just a student. Now you tell us she's been dissociating. Wandering about town, out of her mind. How is this safe? How is this ethical?"

"Please. If you would just give me a moment to explain."

"I don't see how you can explain this in a way that makes any sense." Mike was getting louder, his fists bunched up at his sides. "Are you charging her, too? How much is she paying you?"

"My services are on a sliding scale," Naomi said. "But right now Kate hasn't paid me anything. We've been doing this for free."

"But why?" I asked.

"Because I'm writing my thesis on dissociative disorders," she said. "And you said you were interested in working with me."

"You think she has one of these disorders?" Mike asked.

"I do think so, yes," she replied.

"But why?"

"Because when Kate comes to visit me, she isn't Kate," Naomi explained. "Every time we've sat down to have a discussion, she's presented as an alter, Veronica."

Hearing my other name sent shockwaves through me. I had read it before, in the journal, but Naomi saying the name out loud hit me hard. I floated outside of my body, as though I were a ghost watching events unfold around me. I could feel the smooth leather of the couch underneath my palms, but it felt far away somehow. Naomi and Mike were speaking, but their voices sounded muffled.

"Kate?" Naomi said. "Are you all right?"

Mike wrapped his hand around mine.

"I think she's dissociating," Naomi said. Her voice, for some reason, was loud and clear now. "Kate, why don't you take a few deep breaths? Like this. One…two…three. Just listen to my voice. Relax. Deep breath in…slow exhale."

After a few minutes of breathing exercises, my head cleared. My shoulders relaxed. The tension that had been building in my chest dissipated.

Naomi smiled at me warmly. "There. Welcome back."

"Thank you for helping me with that," I said. "You're good at it."

"Only because we've done it before," Naomi said. "We've had practice, remember?"

I tried to remember. Mike watched me intently. I could almost feel the stress rolling off him in waves. I appreciated his concern, but it was difficult to remember anything with him watching me like a hawk.

"Is there something we can take home for more information?" I asked, sensing we had probably overstayed our welcome. I had all but fainted in her living room just now.

"I'll send you some links," Naomi said. "I've sent them to

Veronica before, but it'll be good for you to have them, too, Kate."

Mike stiffened up at the name Veronica. I noticed, but didn't say anything.

"Thank you," I said to Naomi. "I appreciate you taking the time to talk to us today. I suppose I'll be seeing you again soon."

Naomi smiled, and she seemed to relax knowing we were leaving. Her obvious anxiety made me wonder what kinds of things I told her during our sessions to make her so uptight. "Yes, see you soon."

Once Mike and I were back in the car, he exploded. "Did you hear her? She's insane! Talking to you as if you were a whole other person. It makes no sense. Kate, we have to get you to a real doctor. This one isn't going to work."

I pursed my lips. "She seems nice."

"Nice? Try delusional! If you really do have this disorder, babe, you have to deal with it the right way. I can't believe you went to her and she let you wander around the city dissociated like that! You need to be on medication. As soon as possible."

I wasn't certain if he was right. I seemed to have built a good rapport with Naomi—good enough that she let me come over to her house unscheduled and last minute. She had greeted me like a friend, not just a patient. And she knew me, or at least the "me" I presented to her when I went to her sessions. Who was to say a medical doctor would do the right thing just by throwing pills at me?

I decided to stay silent. Mike was driving, and I didn't want to give him road rage on top of the stress he was already experiencing. I didn't want to start an argument, not when things had already been so up in the air.

When I got home, I had a cold shower. I wanted to wash away all the difficult thoughts and feelings this had brought up. I closed my eyes and let the water rush over me. I tried to think of Veronica. I reached out to her in my mind. But it all seemed for nothing—I had no idea what I was doing. I didn't know how to "contact" her, outside of writing in the journal we shared.

What I desperately wanted to tell her was to stay away for a while, at least for Mike's sake. He was not handling this well, and I didn't want to black out while I was with him only to wake up several hours later with him either angry or concerned.

"Please, just don't make my life harder than it needs to be," I whispered to myself.

There was no answer.

Chapter Two

November 2022

When I finally did hear from Veronica, it wasn't as I expected. I was working on a new song. I needed a pen to write down the notes. I couldn't find one. Nor could I find a blank sheet of paper—each one I pulled up from the catastrophe on my desk was filled with ink already. It had only been a few days, but I had managed to mess it up again.

I opened the journal I shared with Veronica. I flipped to a blank page. I scribbled out notes on the lined paper, humming a tune as I went. I could imagine which instruments would join in the melody. It would begin with piano, and as the music swelled, violins and cellos would be added to the mix. It was the beginning of what would likely become a movie score.

This was when I felt her at the edge of my consciousness. Veronica. I froze and blinked. She wasn't really in the apartment, but it *seemed* like she was. My brain was giving me two different images—one of a raven-haired woman with dark-red lipstick and a pantsuit sitting on my couch, and another where I was entirely alone.

"Maybe if you cleaned up in here a bit more, finding a pen wouldn't have been so difficult," Veronica quipped from where she sat on the couch.

A man appeared beside her. He was in his early thirties, with a beard and curly hair. He wore a gray T-shirt and cargo pants. I recognized him immediately as my childhood imaginary friend, Jeremy. Jer for short.

"If you're so worried about how clean the place is, why don't you hire her a maid?" he asked Veronica.

"A maid?" Veronica repeated. "Where would we get the money for that?"

"Maybe we should be quiet," Jer said. "She's trying to work."

"Work." Veronica sniffed. "When's the last time we made actual money from our music?"

"Hey," Jer said in warning. "It's not like she's making *nothing*. She still gets royalties from the songs she sold."

"Mhm. And that was, what? Two years ago?" Veronica shook her head. "Not good."

"Always the critic, Veronica."

"I came here to talk." She looked at me. "So, are we going to talk?"

"How am I seeing you right now?" I asked.

Veronica sneered. "You mean you don't remember?"

"Go easy," Jer warned. He looked at me with kind eyes. "Naomi explained that we have psychosis. Which explains why you can 'see' us instead of just 'hearing' us in your head."

I sat down on the couch, staying away from Veronica even though I knew she wasn't actually there. I wasn't comfortable being too close to her, especially when she seemed ready to verbally lash out at me.

"What did you want to talk about?" I asked her hesitantly.

"I want more time on the outside," she said. "I didn't get enough recently."

"I don't get *any* time on the outside, but you don't hear me complaining," Jer said.

"I don't understand," I said. "How can I trust you?"

"You can trust us, because we're a part of you," Jer said. "You recognize me, right?"

"Yeah," I said. "I've known you my entire life. It's her who doesn't exactly fit."

"We haven't possessed you or invaded your mind," Veronica said. "We've always been here. Pieces of you. When you black out, one of us takes over. I've been attending therapy sessions for us and speaking for both of you. You were too anxious to go yourself."

"So those five hours I lost…"

"I lived them," Veronica said.

I covered my face with my hands. "This is too much."

"We can go away, if you like," Jer offered.

"No." I was determined now they were here to keep them. "I need to talk to you both. If this is the reality of my life, I need to face it."

"Finally," Veronica sighed. "Something you've said that I agree with."

"I don't like blacking out. And it seems you're the reason this is happening."

She rolled her eyes. "If only you were present during our therapy sessions. It might help if you actually show up to one of those, you know. You'd realize I'm *definitely* not the reason this is all happening."

"Then why?" I asked.

Jer moved closer to me and took my hand. "It's a difficult thing to answer."

"Not *that* difficult," Veronica muttered.

He ignored her. "You experienced this before. Many times. But never connected the dots."

"How could I have blacked out and not noticed?" I asked.

"It isn't always as extreme as blacking out," he said. "Sometimes it's feeling outside of your body, or like the things around you aren't real."

"And you both know why it happens?" I asked.

Jer nodded, slowly. Veronica kept her gaze directed toward her perfectly manicured nails.

"Will you tell me?" I asked.

"It has to do with what happened when you were young."

I sat back in shock. Ah. Now it made sense. The blackouts. The broken psyche. Seeing things, hearing things. Inventing, almost, entire people who didn't exist.

"I don't like to think of that time," I mumbled.

"No shit," Veronica said. "Your avoidance of the topic is what's made things so unstable lately. And this is why I think I should be on the outside more."

"How can you talk to me like that, when you know exactly what happened?" I asked.

"Because it's time to move on," she said. "I've been doing my best to help you with that. Holing up in your apartment and writing music isn't going to heal you."

"Then what will?" I asked.

"Talking to us helps," Jer offered. "Although some conversations are more helpful than others."

"And are you willing to help me, too?" I asked Veronica.

"Of course I am," she shot back. "I might be frustrated with how you've been living our life, but I still care about you."

"She doesn't say that often," Jer admitted.

Although it was my first time meeting her, I knew it was true.

"If you're willing to help me, then please, let's try to be kinder to each other."

"I'll do my best," she said reluctantly.

"Thank you," I said.

When I blinked, they were both gone. I had a sense of fullness inside my head, aware for the first time of their presence alongside my own mind. It was as if three souls inhabited one body. Their voices were like whispers at the back of my mind—not as loud as when they were sitting in front of me.

I collapsed onto the couch, alone. I considered calling Mike and asking him to come see me. But given how he felt about all the dissociation, I didn't want to bother him. I considered journaling, but I didn't want Veronica striking out what I wrote, or tearing out the page, if I wrote about them. It seemed like she wanted the journal to belong to her, and her alone.

I considered what my alters (as Naomi had called them) had told me. The dissociation happened because of things that happened in my past. Tears pricked my eyes. I buried my face in a pillow. I didn't want to think about it. Life was tough enough as it was—why would I turn back and look to the past I had tried so hard to forget?

Veronica had a point. I tended to get caught up in the turmoil of my younger life. It would be better to move forward and leave the past behind. I could see now why letting her go "on the outside" would be more appealing for all of us. If Veronica was living my life for me, she would definitely do a better job of dealing with the trauma.

It felt like sirens were going off in my head. I pulled at my hair. I needed to make it stop.

I grabbed my phone and turned on my favorite playlist. It was mostly folk and indie music. Sad stuff. But it helped me process my feelings. I cried into my hands as the music played. A woman sang softly, and I tried to practice the breathing exercises I had done with Naomi when Mike and I had visited. Inhale…hold it…big exhale. Again.

I wanted to work. To get back to writing music. I was depleted of energy, though, and right now wasn't the time for making progress. Instead, I pressed pause on the playlist and moved slowly over to my piano. I turned it on and placed my hands gently on the keys.

I could tell the piano the things I couldn't tell anyone else. Even myself.

*

The next time I saw Mike, he was dressed in fresh, clean dress pants and a black dress shirt, with a new brown coat that fell past his knees. He had gotten a haircut and a shave. He looked good—put together. The very opposite of how I felt. I was dimly aware of how unkempt I looked in comparison. My hair was pulled up into a messy bun, and I was wearing pajama bottoms and a Buffy T-shirt.

He greeted me with a kiss. "Hey, babe."

"Hi," I replied. "I didn't know you were coming over today. Otherwise, I would have made myself look a bit more presentable."

"Don't worry about it, it isn't even noon yet, anyway," he said. "You're good."

I wasn't certain if I was reading too far into it, but I could hear an edge of anxiety in his voice. The way he was overly primped also made me suspicious. Usually when he showed up looking like that, it was because we were going out on a date. We had no plans today, so I figured that meant he was preparing for something and had given himself a haircut as a way to hype himself up.

"Is everything okay?" I asked.

"Actually, I'm a little messed up," he confessed. "It's the dissociation stuff. I wasn't sure who I would find when you opened the door today."

"It's always me," I said weakly. "I'm still the same person."

"Are you?" he laughed, shortly, but there was no humor in it. "According to your therapist, you don't even go by Kate when you see her. You use a different name entirely. How many other people know Veronica, when I don't?"

"You seem upset," I remarked.

"You're right," he said. "I *am* upset. Or something like it. I don't know entirely what I'm feeling. But I'm not okay. I mean, how do I know that when we're together, I've been with you? And not someone else?"

I blinked. "What?"

"How do I know that when I kiss you, it's you?" he asked. "How do I know that when I hold your hand, it's you? And most importantly, how can I ever tell who I'm talking to?"

"I'm still me, baby. I'm still Kate. I'm just going through something."

"You're Kate, until you're not."

Anger flashed within me briefly, and I sensed Veronica at the edge of my consciousness. I pushed it back, with a conscious effort from who I recognized as Jer in my head.

"I'm always Kate," I said.

"That's not what your therapist said." He shook his head. "And that's another thing. Have you called your doctor yet? You need professional help, not just some random student working on a thesis."

"I think I can make that decision," I said softly. When Mike's tone rose, mine quieted.

I pulled on Jer's presence in my mind. I placed my hands on either side of his shoulders. "I know this is stressful for both of us. But I'm still me, and I still love you." I swallowed, hard. "I just need help."

"I'm so glad to hear you say that." He pulled me into a hug. "You do need help, Kate. You do. You really do. And I'm glad you know that. I hope you find it. Soon."

I pressed my face into the crook of his neck. I felt empty. Usually, when Mike pulled me into a hug, I felt warm and safe. Now I was hollow. I knew he was touching me, but it didn't feel right.

I stepped back and sat down on the couch. Mike followed.

"Have you been working on your music?" he asked.

"A bit," I replied. "I've been playing the piano, mostly. The writing hasn't been easy. Not with everything that's going on."

Mike narrowed his eyes. "Have you been dissociating again?"

I remembered the day before, when I had seen Jer sitting exactly where he was now on the couch.

"A bit," I confessed.

I considered telling him about the psychosis but knew it would worry him unnecessarily. It was bad enough that I dissociated and forgot who and where I was—if I told him I was seeing and hearing things that weren't there, too, he would probably flip out.

"What does 'a bit' mean? Like you only blacked out for half

the time?" he asked.

"No, I mean that I've been feeling...off. Like I'm disconnected from reality."

Concern flooded Mike's features. "That's not good."

"Don't worry," I said.

This was clearly the wrong thing to say.

"How can you tell me not to worry when you're like this?" he asked. "Of course I'm going to worry! My girlfriend is..." He caught himself, but there was a guilty look in his eyes.

"No, go ahead," I said. "Say what you were going to say."

"My... No, it was not nice."

"Say it."

Mike took a deep breath. "I was going to say, how am I meant to be calm when my girlfriend is out of it?"

"You weren't going to say 'out of it.' You were going to say 'crazy.'"

"Kate..." he began, but the familiar flash of anger grew to a roar inside me.

Veronica was close to being on the outside and I didn't want that to happen.

"I think I need time alone," I said. "Thank you for visiting today, but I don't think I can talk about this anymore."

He scoffed. "You're throwing me out? But why? I'm trying to help you."

"I'm not throwing you out. I'm asking you to leave." I tightened my jaw. "Politely."

"What, and you could be less polite, is that what you're saying?"

"I could be." There was a bite in my tone that I didn't recognize. This anger, this rage—it wasn't mine. It felt unfamiliar. I couldn't control it. My fingers trembled. I sat on my hands to stop the movement. "I don't want to have to be, though. So, if you could just leave of your own free will…"

"What the hell?" Mike snapped. "You just told me a few minutes ago you wanted help, and now you're kicking me out?"

"I'm dealing with you accordingly," I said, and that's when I realized how dissociated I already was. Mike's face was clear in front of me, clearer than it had ever been. I noticed things I didn't usually notice, like the freckles around his nose, or the gold circling his pupil. He was in hyper-focus, yet I felt none of those warm and familiar emotions I usually had when looking at him. Instead, I was overwhelmed by anger. I wanted to scream at him and tell him to leave—but instead I remained quiet, and all that agitated energy coalesced.

"Kate, I think you should—"

"Get out!" I exclaimed. I couldn't hold it in any longer. My anger came flooding out, and I lost myself in it, uncertain which parts were me and which parts were Veronica. "I don't want you here, and you're of no help to me at all."

"Don't say that." Mike's mouth sloped downward. "I've been doing my absolute best to help you."

"Oh yeah? So, telling me my therapist sucks and I'm doing everything wrong is helping?" I could hear my voice, but it was Veronica speaking through me. I was within, no longer on the outside, a prisoner in my own mind, watching things unfold.

"I only told you that so you would see a real doctor," he said. "You have to recognize that some of this is insane."

"Of course you would say that—you make snap judgments. You met my therapist for a few minutes at her home, and now you think you know her. You haven't even bothered to ask if I'd like you to sit in on a session."

"But when you're in sessions, you're not Kate. You're…" He

paused, looking me up and down. Realization dawned on him. "Veronica."

"That's right." My features readjusted, settling into a harsher, more critical face. Veronica's face. "And what's so bad about Veronica, anyway? Have you even bothered to try to get to know her? No! You decide that the best thing to do is to take pills and drown out the voices. Well, have you ever considered that the voices might have something important to say?"

He grimaced and stood. "I'm not having this conversation with you."

"Why?" I asked. "Because you're scared I might be right?"

"Because you're being rude. And you're not being yourself right now."

"I'm more myself now than I ever have been!" I yelled. "You just don't care to even meet me. You'd rather shove me back into my glass prison where I remain invisible."

"Is that what you think? That you're in prison?" His eyes had a heavy look to them, as if he hadn't slept. "Is that what our relationship is like to you?"

"I've considered you a threat from the moment I met you. I just hoped I would never have to say it."

There was a beat. Mike buttoned up his coat. "Then I'll go."

I knew I should apologize, but I did nothing. I remained seated on the couch. My entire body trembled now, not just my hands.

Mike opened his mouth to say more but clearly thought better of it. He turned on his heels and slammed the door shut behind him when he left.

I checked the time—12:30 p.m.

I remained seated like that, unmoving, until 2:30 p.m. By then, the shaking had stopped. A war waged in my head, between who would be on the outside now. Veronica had managed to shove me aside, but I was still there. It wasn't as easy for her to take control right now—not as easy as when I blacked out.

When the dissociation lifted, it was like someone had lit a fire nearby. My limbs warmed, and my emotions returned in full force. The strongest feeling was guilt. The second strongest was shame. I was ashamed of how I had spoken to Mike. I had told him he was a threat, instead of the person I loved most in the world. He had been nervous to come see me, expecting me to be volatile, and I had proved him right.

I picked up my journal.

Maybe I do really need a medical doctor.

"No!" I heard Veronica say. She wore a different outfit now: a black A-line dress. Her hair was pulled up, like mine, but somehow, she made it look intentional. "We don't need a doctor. Naomi is helping us just fine."

"Naomi is *not* helping us just fine," I shot back. "What was that? You ran him out of our place!"

"I needed to; you were sweating under the pressure!" Veronica shot back.

"I was being *careful* with my language, something you could learn a thing or two about."

"Why would I need to be careful with him? He's a grown man, for God's sake!"

"He's a human being. With feelings, just like you and me!"

I caught a glimpse of myself in the mirror hanging on the wall opposite me. I was alone in my apartment, arguing with the air. But it felt so real. A moment later, the illusion grabbed hold of me again, and tightly this time.

"He's trying to stop me from having a voice," Veronica said. "Just like the last one did."

"What do you mean? I never blacked out with my exes."

"That's what you think," she commented cryptically.

"Are you kidding me? This has been going on for longer than I thought?"

"Longer than the time we've known Naomi, yes."

"Where's Jer when you need him?" I asked.

"You don't *need* him right now," Veronica snapped. "Stop using him as a crutch."

"So how long have you been in my head?" I asked.

"You really don't remember? Wow, I would say I'm insulted, but I guess I would expect nothing less from the side of our personality that runs and hides when things get messy."

"We're the same person," I ground out in frustration. "I don't see how criticizing me is going to get you anywhere in this argument."

"Oh." She laughed. "You think this is an argument. That's cute. No, believe me, when we have one of those, you will know."

"Okay, point taken," I said. "So, when did all of this start?"

Veronica crossed her arms in front of her chest. "When we were ten."

"That's twenty years ago."

"Yep."

"So, you've been…what, coexisting with me all this time without me knowing it?"

"I wouldn't say you were completely unaware, not at first. You knew who I was, and back then, you actually liked me." Now it was Veronica who looked tired. I could sense her anger subduing, turning into something far closer to exhaustion. "Back when we were kids."

"I don't remember."

"Again, I'm not surprised. You used to think of Jer and me

as imaginary friends. And then later you called us angels. But we were always there, one way or another."

"And now I can see you standing in front of me."

She outstretched her arms. "Here I am."

Tears threatened to spill from my eyes. "Why won't you leave me alone?"

"Because you need me. You've always needed me. You just don't realize it yet." She pressed a palm to her chest. "I'm just as necessary as Jer is. You only like him because he's always had a soft spot for you. Always wanted to be gentle. I tried that, for a while, and I saw where it got us. Nowhere good. So, for your own benefit, I'm hard on you. That's just the way it has to be."

"Is that what our therapist said, too?" I asked. "That I'm hopeless? A lost cause? That I'm not even worth trying to be kind to?"

"Of course not," Veronica said. "She wants all of us to live in harmony. She thinks it's possible."

"With or without medication?" I asked.

"I don't want to have that conversation again. I told you already, pills will just shut me up. Imprison me further in this body that I don't even own. Why would you want to do that to me?"

"Why doesn't Jer seem as bothered by the idea? If it's so horrible."

"Because he never had goals and aspirations like I do!" she said. "I've had so many dreams for the future, and I've had to sit on the sidelines and watch you mess it all up every step of the way!"

"God, I really must have disappointed you."

For a moment, she worried her lip, and regret shone in her eyes. Still, she said, "It was bound to happen eventually."

"I need help. You can either support me, or you can leave.

Just like Mike did."

Veronica hesitated.

"If you're not going to help, then leave!" I yelled.

She was gone. I lay back down on the couch. Mike might not be right about everything. Veronica may even have a point about her right to a voice. But one thing was certain: I couldn't continue living like this. It was impacting not only my ability to write music (and make a living) but my ability to have a normal conversation with the person I loved most in the world. I couldn't even have a civil conversation with myself.

I knew it was time for a change.

Chapter Three

November 2022

I decided to meet with my best friend Brielle. She always had great insights into my personal life, and I often went to her when I felt lost. I knew she would be intrigued by all the drama with Mike. I needed a large dose of sympathy right now, and I knew she would be able to provide it.

We met at our favorite lunch spot, Shelby's. The sign was painted pastel blue with white lettering. The inside of the cafe was like an old-timey diner. I found Brielle sitting in a booth with her purse on the table next to her. Her auburn hair was slicked back and fell over her shoulders. Her ears were adorned with several new piercings. Her short-sleeved shirt showed off her tattooed arms.

"Kate!" She stood and hugged me as soon as I got to the booth. "It's so nice to see you."

I let out a sigh of relief when she wrapped her arms around me. "You have no idea how much I needed this today."

"Have things been that rough?" she asked, taking her seat.

"Incredibly rough," I replied, sitting down.

"Does it have to do with Mike?"

"Partly. But a lot of it just has to do with how convoluted everything is in my head."

"Let's get you some food," she said. "And then I want to hear all about it."

The waitress came to take our orders. I got French toast with strawberries. Brielle got a veggie omelet with extra cheese. We both ordered mango smoothies. Those came out right away from the kitchen.

"Drink up," Brielle said. "You're going to need all the energy you can get to tell me this story. I can already tell."

"Is it that obvious?" I took a sip of my smoothie.

"Painfully. I can tell when something's bothering you. Your shoulders get all tense. And your voice changes."

"It does? How?"

"It gets a little deeper, believe it or not."

My face grew hot. "I didn't know that."

"Point is, I know when something is bothering you. So go on. You can tell me what's happening."

"Where to start?" I sighed. "Mike and I got into a fight."

"About what?"

"My health."

"Why would you fight about that? Are you okay? Is something going on that I should know about? Oh, sorry. That's a lot of questions. I should let you answer first."

"I've been dissociating lately. Do you know what that means?"

"I've heard of it before, during one of my psych classes in university," she replied. "But what does it mean for you?"

"For me, I kind of black out. And it turns out I act like a completely different person when I do." I pushed my smoothie away, nauseated. Maybe lunch hadn't been the best setting for this conversation, given the tumultuous emotions I felt inside.

"And how does this connect to the fight with Mike?" she asked.

We paused as the waitress arrived with our food. We both thanked her. When she was out of earshot, we continued our conversation.

"Mike tried to help me connect the dots. Figure out what I've been experiencing. But things got messy. I got mad at him. I yelled at him and told him to leave my apartment. We haven't spoken since."

"And when was that?"

"Four days ago."

Brielle sucked in a breath. "That's rough."

"Yeah, I'd say."

"Have you tried reaching out to him?"

"Yes. I've tried calling, texting. I've done everything except show up at his place and try to knock down the door."

She took a bite of her omelet. "Is that option being considered?"

"Only a little bit, when I'm feeling desperate to get back in touch with him. I don't want to bother him, though. And he clearly wants to be left alone. No amount of apologizing for what I said can actually take back the words."

"No, I guess not. But what did you say that was so unforgivable?"

"I told him I thought he was a threat to me from the day I

met him, and this hasn't changed."

"Wow, harsh. But I assume you must've had a good reason for saying something like that."

"I don't know if reason really comes into it. It was all dissociation and emotion. I felt like I was being controlled by someone else."

"Have you talked to someone about this? Like, a professional?"

"Apparently, I've been going to a therapist for the last little while. Mike thinks it's not enough, though. He wants me to see a doctor. I'm starting to agree. I've been…seeing things."

"Things that aren't there?" Brielle asked.

"Yeah."

"Damn. That's serious. Have you been hearing things, too, or just seeing them?"

"The whole thing. Hearing, seeing. Feeling, even."

She shivered. "That's spooky. I'm so sorry, Kate. It sounds like you need help. I don't know where from."

"I've only just come into contact with this side of me. I'm scared that if I take medication, it will cut off the voices completely, and I'll never be able to figure out what's going on with me. My therapist has been working with me to uncover the things I've forgotten. All those times I visited her, I dissociated and acted as someone else. As Veronica. That's the name I use when I'm not myself."

"Veronica," Brielle repeated, as if testing out the name. "I guess you could look like a Veronica."

"What about Jeremy?" I asked. "Because that's the name of the other person I see."

Brielle looked to either side of me. "Are…Veronica and Jeremy here with us now?"

"Not exactly. They're in my mind, always, and I can feel them to a certain extent—even hear them—but I don't see them right now."

"Why's that? Why do you think sometimes you can see them and hear them, and then other times they're just there in your head?"

"I think stress has to do with it," I said. "It seems like when I'm freaked out, they show up."

"Will you go back to the therapist? You seem to think she's been helpful."

"Yeah, she does seem helpful, but I don't remember our sessions together. I only have a brief meeting to go off."

Brielle tapped her fingers on the table. She was a drummer. When she was anxious, she made a rhythm. "Have I ever met Veronica?"

"It's possible," I replied. "Apparently this has been going on for far longer than I even knew."

"Wow." She paused. "So, it's possible that sometimes when we've been hanging out, you've been dissociated and acting like a completely different person. Well, that explains why you seem…different, when you're stressed out. I figured it was just an effect of your personality." She laughed. "I'm your best friend, and I had no idea this was going on."

"Don't feel bad. It was happening to me, and *I* had no idea what was going on."

"I know, I just always prided myself on being observant, especially when it came to the people closest to me. Now I can't exactly claim to be the most observant person in the world."

"You noticed differences in me when I was stressed. That's more than I did."

"Would I be able to talk to them?" Brielle asked. "These…

other people in your head. Or is it only you who can talk to them?"

I felt warmth spread through me. I was grateful to have a friend like Brielle, who not only engaged with me on the topic, but was willing to learn more. Even if it was unorthodox. I loved her free, creative spirit—and how it didn't stop her from asking the hard-hitting questions.

"I don't know," I admitted. "I've only tried to talk to Veronica outside of an episode once. Otherwise, it only seems to work when I'm dissociated."

"Want to try now?" she asked. "Maybe I can get to know her. Hear a little from her side. Since she has things to say."

I focused on the feeling in my head of her presence. I could picture her perfectly, although it wasn't like when I was hallucinating. In my mind, she was as churlish as usual. It didn't seem like she wanted to talk. I reached out for Jer in my mind. I could sense his calming influence.

I cleared my throat. This felt oddly performative, but I didn't know how else to go about it. It was definitely an interesting thought experiment. And being able to summon my alters on command would be helpful for processing whatever issues were being left untreated.

Despite my efforts, however, nothing happened.

"I don't think it works that way," I said. "I can...feel them here, in my mind, but it's not like I can just let them take over."

"Can you like, talk to them?" she asked.

"Yeah, in my head."

"Can I ask what Veronica thinks of me?"

I paused. I reflected on the thought. I could hear Veronica's words right away. I relayed them to Brielle. "She says you're a good friend who has always been there for us. She trusts you more than Mike."

"Poor Mike. But I get it. Right now, you two are fighting, so he seems like the villain."

"I hope he forgives me soon. I don't know how many more times I can text him while keeping my dignity intact."

"He'll talk when he's ready," she said. "You've texted and called him, true. But you haven't done what he suggested yet—see a doctor."

I dropped my gaze to my lap. That unfamiliar sound of sirens went off in my head again. "You're right. I'm scared to start medication, but I don't want fear to control me."

Brielle reached across the table and squeezed my hand. "I'm here for you, okay? You're not alone. And Mike will come around. You'll see. Your people are here for you."

I forced a smile for her. "Thank you."

*

Instead of going directly to a doctor, I requested an appointment with Naomi. It was the first appointment where I would be going as Kate, not Veronica. I figured if anyone could tell me whether I needed to be on medication, it would be her. I was afraid of the sedating effects that many psychiatric meds had. I wanted help with the dissociation and distress—but I didn't want to lose who I was.

Naomi greeted me cheerfully at the door when I arrived at her place. She did all her sessions here, which I found odd, but it likely saved her on renting office space.

"Nice to see you again," Naomi said. "Please, make yourself comfortable. I'll go fetch us a pot of tea."

I sat down on the couch, feeling small on it now without Mike by my side. I tried to recall the times I had been here before, but my memories were hazy. I focused on the small details of the room. The scent of vanilla wafting through the air—likely a candle in the kitchen. That reminded me of something, and I had a flash of memory spark through my mind. I was wearing a summer dress and flip-flops. But the memory was gone almost as fast as it came up. I looked around the room for something else that might trigger a memory. Naomi had a bookcase sitting behind her chair with a few books on trauma and healing.

Trauma. That would surely bring back memories and was probably something I had already talked to Naomi about at length. Veronica and Jer had mentioned that my dissociation had to do with what happened when I was young. A topic I avoided desperately. But it seemed if I wanted to connect with my alters, and the rest of my psyche, I would have to face it.

I tried to steady my breath. Naomi came back into the living room carrying two cups of tea. She placed mine in front of me. I noted that it had exactly the right amount of milk—she knew how I liked my tea. She was observant, and I liked that.

"What brings you in today, Kate?" Naomi asked.

"I need to remember things," I said. "My boyfriend thinks the best way to handle all of this is to take medication and make it all go away. I'm afraid of losing myself, though. So, I need to find a way to get back to myself without also losing most of the things I need to remember."

"Losing yourself," Naomi repeated. "Yes, you've mentioned being afraid of this before. When you were presenting to me as Veronica. She's quite concerned about not being heard."

I nodded. "She's told me as much."

"And do you think she has a valid point? That she deserves to be heard?"

"I think she's getting in the way quite a lot lately," I said. Tears filled my eyes. "It's been five days now since I've spoken to

Mike, because of her...because of my anger."

"You got into a fight?"

"Yes. I dissociated a bit and yelled at him. Well, Veronica yelled at him. I don't know the difference anymore. We're the same person, after all."

"In a way, yes," she said. "But when you're here with me, for our purposes, we'll say you're two different people. With different desires, goals, ambitions, and emotions. It'll help you process it."

"Veronica told him he was a threat to us. I don't know where that line of reasoning came from. I've never seen him that way."

"It might help if you can understand Veronica's motivations. She must have a reason for her opinion."

"Maybe because most men can't be trusted," I said hesitantly.

"Do you believe that?"

"A bit."

"Why's that?"

"Because of what happened to me when I was young."

Naomi nodded, as if she had expected this to come up. "We don't have to talk about it, if you don't want to. Say whatever you're comfortable with."

"I was...hurt." I paused, looking at Naomi. She didn't smile, but she didn't look surprised either. Instead, she listened patiently.

"You've spoken of this before," Naomi said. "But Veronica usually steered away from the memory. You've done a great job so far."

I cried. Naomi offered me tissues.

"It's all right," she said, her tone as soft as the tissues. "You've spoken about it and told me it happened. That's a step in the right direction."

"But I always avoid the hardest parts," I said, anger rising within me.

"We can take it as slow as you like," Naomi assured me. "It's okay that you can't talk about it all yet."

I sniffed. "Thank you."

Although I was thankful for her insight as a therapist, I was left feeling disoriented, confused, and distraught.

"I can see that you're still feeling quite a bit of anxiety," she observed. "Would it help if we did a breathing exercise together?"

I nodded. She instructed me to take a deep breath in through my nose, and exhale through my mouth. We did this together for a minute or so, and my body began to relax. The anger within me dampened somewhat. It was still there, sitting in my belly, but it wasn't roaring up into my chest anymore.

"I feel a bit better," I said.

"May I ask how the rest of you are feeling right now?" Naomi asked.

"I can feel Veronica's anger inside of me. Although it's not anger about the attack. It's anger at me. For avoiding the topic. For not being able to tell the whole story."

"That's okay," Naomi said softly. "And Jeremy?"

"He's sad. He wishes this was easier for me. But he's willing to help me through it. To coach me through the memories."

"Then, if you're willing, try to remember. When did Veronica and Jer first appear in your life?"

I thought for a moment. "I remember Jer being there when I was eleven. Life started changing around then."

"How so?"

I bit my lip. Had Veronica not told her this already? Why did I need to repeat it all? It was such an uncomfortable topic, but I knew I wouldn't get better if I didn't talk about it.

"Things got violent at home," I said. "And I sought refuge in the wrong places."

"Do you want to share more about how this happened?"

"It was my father." My stomach lurched, as though I were falling from up high. I felt as if something weighed down my tongue, making it difficult to speak. "He was abusive."

"How was he abusive?" Naomi asked.

"He would hit me, sometimes. Mostly when he was drunk. But the punches would hurt less than…" I was choking up, like there was a vice around my neck.

"Less than what?"

"They hurt less than his words," I said.

"He spoke badly to you?"

Jer appeared beside me on the couch. He reached out and held my hand. "You can do it. It's okay. You can trust Naomi. And he's not here anymore. It's just you and me."

"Yes," I said. "He'd put me down a lot. Say that I was cursed. That I was an evil being. But Jer was always there, by my side."

"Would Jer take care of you, during these moments?" Naomi asked.

"Yes. He would always say, 'It's you and me now.'"

"So, you were in it together."

"Yeah." I wiped my eyes. "Jer would sit with me when Dad would put me down. He'd call me all sorts of things. Tell me I was a loser, that I was worth nothing. That I was repulsive and would never have any friends." I bit back a sob. "There were days I was relieved to receive my punishments in silence. At least then the words couldn't cut through me."

"That's very brave of you to share," Naomi said.

I didn't feel brave though. I felt like a scared little girl.

"Just you and me," Jer said, and it was reassuring. Warmth

spread from my fingertips all the way to my chest. Even when the worst emotions and memories were crashing against my psyche in waves, I was never alone.

"I think Jer first appeared because I needed a friend."

"Not only a friend, but a protector," Naomi said. "Think of how the brain responds to trauma. You were so young. You needed a protector. From what I can guess, your mom didn't step in to save you from your father. So, your mind did something incredible. It created that support you needed. In this case, it took the form of Jer."

"And what about Veronica?" I asked. "Why did *she* appear? Why did I need to create a version of me that was so critical?"

"Veronica serves a different purpose. Can you think of your earliest memory of her?"

I looked at Jer. "I don't know. It's hard to remember."

"Try," he said. "Think about when you would get angry."

Anger. That seemed to be an emotion that was inextricably linked with Veronica. She was always so angry, all the time, and at everything—whether it was my career choice, my love life, or anything else. But the roots of this anger went far deeper than all those seemingly superficial things. And it led me to the anger I had buried down, deep down.

"When I would get angry, Veronica would appear," I said. "Sometimes in my mind, and sometimes in my voice. I don't think I recognized it when she took over. But I would be like a different person."

"Do you recall blacking out at all?"

"No," I said. "But I remember feeling outside of my body. I remember watching little me yell at my father. I remember one night in his drunken stupor, he just stared at me. Literally gaping. He couldn't believe that I had the nerve to talk back to him."

"What did you say to your father that shocked him so much?" Naomi asked.

"I told him if he ever laid a hand on me again, I would..." I stopped. I had never told anyone this before.

"You would do what?" she asked.

Jer nodded his approval. "It's okay, Kate. Go on."

"I told him if he touched me again, I would destroy him."

"Wow." Naomi let her words hang in the air for several moments, her forehead creased with concern. "I can imagine how scared you must have been to threaten something like that."

"I didn't feel scared," I admitted. "I felt powerful. It was the first time in my life that I was able to stand up for myself."

"What happened after that?"

"He left me alone. The threat was too real for him to not believe me. I was such an angry teenager, always fighting with my parents. But the older I got, the scarier I got, too. My threats became more and more real. Eventually my father left me alone. He didn't want me fighting back."

"That doesn't mean the hurt wasn't still there," Naomi said.

I shut my eyes. "You're right."

"Is this too much for you?" Naomi asked. "If it is, just let me know, and we'll slow it down."

"It's...a lot," I admitted. I opened my eyes and frowned. "I guess Veronica and Jer really have been there since the beginning. Keeping me safe."

"They have. And if my sessions with Veronica are any indication, they both care for you very deeply. I hope you know that these people you share your mind-space with, they want you to be safe. They don't want you to be back in the situation you were in when you were just a little girl."

I shuddered. "I don't want to be back there again. And I'm

afraid the more I talk, the more I'll go back there in my mind."

"Then we've talked enough," Jer said. "Time for us to cool down. Ask Naomi to do some breathing techniques with you."

"Would we be able to take some deep breaths together?" I asked.

Naomi smiled. "Yes. For sure. Let's do that now. Deep breath in through the nose, and out through the mouth…"

As I followed Naomi's instructions, my body tingled. It was extremely relaxing, and I had no doubt that was the intended effect.

Veronica appeared by my side. She wore a black pencil skirt and a pink silk blouse. She reached out for my hand. I let her take it. I breathed in through my nose and exhaled through my mouth. Both Veronica and Jer held my hands as I relaxed further.

I would never be alone again. I would never have to go back to the state I was in when I was ten.

I had Naomi, with her professional insight and her practiced skills. But I also had my other selves. I had relied on them to get me through the last twenty years. They wouldn't abandon me when I needed them most.

We were in this together.

*

When I got home, I sat down at my desk and started journaling. I wrote about the session with Naomi, how it had gone, and the moments when Jer and Veronica had appeared. I wrote about how it made me feel to talk so openly about my father. It was a topic I had avoided discussing—even Mike knew the bare minimum, and given Veronica's mistrust of him, I could see why we had never shared the details of the abuse I had suffered with him before.

I also knew something else walking away from this therapy appointment. I had barely scratched the surface with Naomi—especially as Kate. Veronica had attended a few sessions, and now it was my turn to try to uncover the truth. To try to find out who I really was. Because right now, I had no idea who Kate Moore was. I thought I knew myself, but now, even my reflection seemed alien to me. I had two whole other personalities who would present themselves at different times, sometimes to a shockingly mind-altering degree. Other times, it was more subtle. But if my personality wasn't stable, how was I meant to know who I was?

This kind of philosophizing would break any academic's head, let alone mine. I wasn't trained in philosophy and decided not to spiral down the rabbit hole of "how can one body possibly host three souls?"

Instead, I tried to focus on my feelings. It had been nice, after all the criticism I had received from Veronica, to finally have a moment of tenderness with her. To bond over our childhood trauma, and to know that even though we might not always see eye to eye, we both cared for each other and didn't want to see the other hurt. Which was a bit dizzying, when I considered we were the same person. It was as Naomi said—for our purposes, in therapy, it helped to think of Veronica and Jer as two separate individuals who were created intentionally.

"You know, therapy was always hard for me," Veronica said, still in the same pencil skirt and blouse she wore during our appointment. She stood by my desk now, her hand placed firmly by my journal, demanding my attention.

"I can see why it would be hard," I said, uncertain why she had suddenly appeared. Usually, Veronica showed up when I was distressed. Now, it made sense. She had been created as a kind of protector, too, although a less motherly one.

"I hope you know that..." Veronica sighed, and a dent appeared above her left eyebrow. "I hope you know that...that..." I waited for her to finish her sentence. She looked away from me. "I hope you know that I'm proud of you. There, I said it."

"Really? Why?"

"You finally did something you were scared to do for decades. You spoke to a professional about what's going on. Granted, she's not a full therapist, but it's a step in the right direction."

"Wow, I don't think I've ever seen you in such a generous mood."

"Don't get used to it," Veronica snapped.

Despite her anger, I smiled. "Thank you for telling me that you're proud. I'm proud of us, too."

Her eyes drifted over to where my phone sat face down on my desk. "So does that mean you'll keep seeing Naomi?"

"I think that would probably be for the best, yeah," I replied.

"And are you going to do what Mike wants?" Veronica asked. "Are you going to talk to a doctor about going on medication?"

I pressed a hand to my brow. "I don't know. I don't think so. There's so much to consider. Medicating myself might slow me down. Might make the hallucinations go away. But I'm making progress here, in therapy. Valuable progress. And Naomi said medication was my choice. Not something I had to do."

"But your boyfriend thinks you have to do it," Veronica said.

"If he's even still my boyfriend," I said lamely. "It's been days since I've heard from him. Maybe he's ghosting me."

She sniffed. "Doubtful. He's just miserable and he's soaking in it. He'll contact you again soon. But the real question is, do you still want anything to do with him?"

"I love him," I shot back. "Of course I want to see him again.

What is your major problem with him, anyway? It seems like you hate him."

"I do hate him," she said simply. "And no, it's not because I'm a lesbian."

That piece of information surprised me. "No way."

"Yes way. And maybe my unique perspective can inform you that he is absolutely not the right guy for you."

"If you're gay, then does that make me…"

"No, you're not a lesbian, dear," Veronica said, her voice almost kind.

"And what about Jer?"

"Straight as a board."

"So that makes me…" I racked my brain for the proper term. What did you call a person with the personalities of both a straight man and a lesbian in her head?

"You might be on some spectrum of bisexuality, but that's up for you to discover," she said.

"I'm not broken up with Mike. There's nothing to discover."

"If you say so."

"Here, I'll call him right now."

Despite how certain I sounded about the stability of my relationship, my thoughts were a tangled mess. What if Mike wasn't right for me anymore? He hadn't accepted my apology, and it's not like I hadn't considered the fact that things might be over between us.

I grabbed my phone and pulled up Mike's number. I pressed call.

"He probably won't pick up," Veronica said.

My chest tightened as the phone rang.

Mike finally answered. "Hello?"

"Hi," I said. "Thought I'd try to check in. We haven't talked in a few days."

"I know, Kate," he said. "That was on purpose."

"I've been really worried," I continued. "You didn't respond to any of my texts or calls. You haven't shown up at my place. I thought maybe you were never going to talk to me again."

Mike sighed. "There's no need to be dramatic. I was going to get back to you."

"When? Because you made no effort to reply to me at all."

"I needed space. Time to think."

"Think about what?" I asked.

"Think about where this is going."

Veronica gave me a pointed look. I pressed on.

"Why does it sound like you're breaking up with me?" I asked.

"We're just talking," he said, but there was a note of annoyance in his tone. "But what did you expect, really? A cheery conversation after you told me to get out of your apartment and called me a threat?"

"I told you over text, I am so, so sorry for that. It wasn't me. I was dissociated. Can't you try to understand that?"

"Don't you think I am? That I've been wrestling with this? I know that illness isn't you, but it's also hard to reconcile. I've been absolutely terrified because you're turning into a person I don't even recognize."

"I'm working on it. I went to therapy."

"*Just* therapy?" Mike asked. "What about going to see a doctor?"

"I'm going to stick with therapy for now," I said. "Naomi's been helping me work through the root causes of what's going on with me."

"And what are those reasons, exactly?"

"Things that happened when I was a kid."

A sensation of fear crept up my neck. I had already gone over the trauma with Naomi—I didn't want to have to do it again with Mike.

There must've been a long pause, because Mike said, "Kate?"

"Yeah, I'm here."

"I don't think this is working out."

"Huh? What isn't working out?"

"This conversation. This whole thing." He took a deep breath. "I hate to say this, but you need to make a decision. Get your life together, or we can't do this."

"What, you mean, take medication or we're done?"

"For your own well-being, you need a real psychiatrist."

"Why can't you accept that I know what's best for me?" I asked.

"Because you don't even know who you are!" Mike exclaimed. "I can't do this. Until you decide to put your health and well-being first, I can't be near you."

"Does this mean you really *are* breaking up with me?"

"Yeah, I guess I am," he said. "I love you so much, and I hate to leave you this way, but consider this a wake-up call. You need to do something about this."

"And I am. I'm working on it. Are you really going to punish me for not moving at a fast enough pace?"

"You're just not getting it. I don't know if you ever will."

"Please," I said weakly. "Please don't leave me. Not now."

"I'm sorry, Kate, but you've given me no other choice." There was a beat. "Goodbye. I hope you choose your health over this."

He hung up.

I threw my phone aside and curled up into a ball on my desk chair. I cried.

Jer rubbed my back. "I'm here for you, honey."

Veronica crossed her arms in front of her chest. She didn't need to say anything—I knew what she was thinking: *I told you so.*

"Could you give us the room?" Jer asked Veronica.

She rolled her eyes. "Fine, whatever."

She vanished. I threw my arms around Jer's neck. He hugged me tightly.

"Just you and me now, girlie," he said. "Just you and me now."

Chapter Four

November 2022

My friend from high school, Phoebe, was coming to town and had invited Brielle and me out to eat. When she came to town, we always got together. We agreed to meet for brunch. I had decided to tell them about Mike and me breaking up. Phoebe was one of my best friends, but she could be a little judgmental at times. I worried she wouldn't understand if I opened up to her about Jer and Veronica.

When I arrived at the restaurant, I spotted Brielle and Phoebe sitting together at a table. Phoebe's brown hair was newly styled into a bob. She was dressed in black leather pants and a long-sleeved black shirt. Around her neck was a choker necklace. She had the goth look down pat. Brielle wore a red-and-black flannel shirt that complimented her hair and jeans. I had on black leggings and a long turquoise shirt. I went over to them.

"Hey guys," I said.

"Hey, Kate!" Brielle said.

"Nice to see you," Phoebe said.

We hugged.

"It's been way too long," I said.

"I know," Brielle agreed. "If only she lived here, we wouldn't have to wait months between visits."

"I might move back one day," Phoebe said. She looked me over quickly. "Say, did you sleep at all last night? You're looking really tired."

There it was. The judgment I had come to expect from Phoebe. I caught my reflection in a mirror hanging opposite our table. She was right. I hated it when she was right. I had dark circles under my eyes that makeup just couldn't conceal.

I sat down. Phoebe followed suit.

"Things have been tough lately," I said.

"Tell us about it," Brielle said. "And don't feel pressured to eat. I know it's brunch, but I also know how nauseated you get when you haven't slept well. I'll never forget our trip to Ireland, when you barely slept a wink on the plane, and then spent the next few hours throwing up because…"

"I ate an apple. I remember." I shook my head. "Please, let's skip the gory details. Especially right before you two are about to eat. But thank you for remembering. I'll probably just get something to drink. I really am under the weather."

"What's going on?" Brielle asked. "Does it have to do with the fight you had with Mike?"

"Yeah," I replied, my voice cracking. "He broke up with me over the phone."

"He did what?" Phoebe asked in disbelief. "Catch me up, girl, because I feel so lost here."

"We've been fighting a lot because I've…" I hesitated, unsure of how to introduce the topic. "I've not been myself lately."

"How could he break up with you, though?" Phoebe asked in disbelief. "I thought you two were so in love."

"So did I," I admitted. "You know, it always seemed so easy. When I was young, all I wanted from a partner was someone who would be nice to me and watch my favorite romance movies with me. When did everything become so hard?"

Brielle patted me sympathetically on the hand. "I hear you, honey."

"Now I have to adjust all of my requirements for a partner," I said. "Finding someone new. But I'm afraid nobody will ever have me."

"Why would you say that?" Phoebe asked. "What could you want that's so unreasonable?"

"I want someone who would spend time with me and be willing to express their feelings. Communication, at the minimum."

"Okay, that all sounds pretty standard," Brielle said.

"But where it gets messy is with my mental illness. How can I expect anyone to be patient and understanding when I'm so very messed up?"

"Oh, darling," Brielle said. "If they're not willing to do that, then they are not meant for you, the same way Mike likely wasn't meant for you."

"I tried to hide myself to make myself likable." I could hear the tears in my voice before they sprang to my eyes. "Why couldn't I just be likable?"

"You are likable," Phoebe said. "How dare he dump you like that. He didn't even bother to show up at your place?"

"No," I said. "He gave me an ultimatum. Told me either I handled my health his way, or he couldn't see me anymore."

"Wait, wait," Phoebe said. "I'm lost. What are you talking about? Are you depressed or something?"

Tongue-tied, I thought of how to respond. I couldn't very well tell her that I hallucinated two individuals. Or that these individuals sometimes took over my body and mind during episodes of dissociation. So, what did I say?

"Not depression," I said. "Nothing extreme. Nothing you need to worry about."

"Okay," Phoebe said slowly. "That isn't exactly reassuring."

"And it's not entirely true that she shouldn't worry," Brielle said. "I've had plenty to worry about with what you told me."

"Okay." I sighed. "Maybe I'm downplaying it a bit. The truth is, Phoebe, I've been blacking out. Forgetting where I am, what I'm doing. And sometimes when I black out, I act like a different person."

"How can you act like a different person?" Phoebe asked.

"I go out and use a different name," I said. "I wear different clothes. I act differently."

"That doesn't make sense," Phoebe said. "You mean you black out and just go about your day acting like someone else?"

"Yeah," I said.

"Sounds…hard." Phoebe went quiet after that. I figured she was processing.

"It is hard. But I'm learning to accept it. Including all of my pieces."

"So, is this like schizophrenia or something?" Phoebe asked.

"We don't have a label yet," I said. "I haven't been diagnosed."

"How can you properly treat it without a diagnosis?" Phoebe asked.

"I've been in therapy," I said.

"And what does the therapist help you with?"

"We talk about the different sides of me. Sometimes, I see and hear things that aren't there. That includes these...people in my head."

Phoebe ran a hand over her face. "This is a lot to take in."

"But we're here for you," Brielle said. "Right, Phoebe?"

"I..." Phoebe stared off toward the kitchen, as if wishing she had an escape route. I had never seen her look so skittish before. "I don't know what to say."

We sat in silence for a few moments, the mood growing increasingly uncomfortable.

Brielle reached out to take my hand. "I think I speak for both of us when I say we know you're going through a terrible time with all this mental health stuff and your breakup with Mike." She looked at Phoebe expectantly. "Right, Phoebes?"

Phoebe shook her head. "I'm sorry, I just can't quite get past the fact that you go out and act like a different person. Are you going to show up to our next brunch wearing a suit and calling yourself a guy's name?"

"What?" My heart slammed in my chest. I had never heard Phoebe talk to me this way, not in our decade of friendship. "No."

"Look, my heart goes out to you for everything that's happened with Mike recently," Phoebe said. "But this dissociation crap? It's crazy. I'm supposed to believe there's all these sides to you that I've never met? Like multiple personalities or something? That's just...so out there, Kate. I can't believe you would spring this on me at our brunch."

"I..." My voice broke slightly. Brielle shot me a worried glance, but I pressed on. "I didn't mean to spring anything on you, I thought I would just share what I've been going through..."

"Well, you did." Phoebe glared at Brielle. "You *both* sprung this on me."

"Why are you talking to me like I'm a villain here?" Brielle asked.

"Because you knew about Kate's situation, and you still thought we could all sit down and have brunch together." Phoebe scoffed. "This is so not what I had in mind. But it's very typical of you, Kate, now that I think about it."

"What? How?" I asked.

"Making it all about you. You couldn't handle having one brunch where things weren't all about you, could you? So, you bring up this wild story hoping to get sympathy from everyone."

"I didn't," I protested. The way Phoebe clenched her jaw told me she wasn't buying it.

"I don't think this is fair at all," Brielle said. "You're being way too harsh on her, Phoebe. Kate doesn't need this right now. She's going through enough."

"Maybe she should have thought about that before dropping a huge bombshell on me!" Phoebe exclaimed. "All Kate can talk about is all her little Kate-problems. It's selfish!"

"I didn't mean to overtake the conversation," I said weakly. "I just thought you'd want an update on how my life was going…"

"Yeah, and it seems to be going pretty badly." Phoebe exhaled. "How am I supposed to react? How did Brielle react? Because clearly, you're so in the right, and I'm so in the wrong."

"Nobody is in the right or the wrong," Brielle replied. "Kate's just trying to let you in on her life a bit. Why are you getting so defensive?"

"I'm not defensive!" Phoebe exclaimed. "I'm just tired of pretending like Kate's life is ending." She looked at me. "You're going through a breakup. That's really hard, and I'm sorry. It sounds like therapy is probably the best thing for you right now, so I'm glad you're seeing someone. But this is not the way to bring it up, and it certainly isn't the right place for it."

"Where would the right place be, then, Phoebes?" Brielle asked. "Because this seems perfectly reasonable to me."

I couldn't speak. My hands trembled. I swallowed, hard. I tried to find my voice, but it was gone. Veronica's anger rose within me, but this definitely wasn't the right time for her to make an appearance and meet Phoebe. I desperately reached out to Jer in my mind, hoping to find his soothing presence.

Just you and me? I thought.

There was no response. As I'd discovered, it wasn't as easy as that to dissociate on command.

I looked at Brielle. At least she was here. At least she was on my side.

"Phoebe, what's really going on?" I asked. "I've never seen you so upset before."

"I'm upset because this is like being brought in on a secret that you two so obviously shared together before you shared it with me," Phoebe said. "I feel completely in the dark here, and you two didn't think to fill me in before I drove all the way here to see your sorry asses."

"Really, there's no need to speak that way," Brielle said quietly. I could tell she was trying to lower the tone of the entire conversation, because Phoebe was getting loud. And when Phoebe got mad, she tended to yell.

I didn't want that to happen. "I'm sorry," was all I managed to say. My voice sounded hoarse. I realized dimly that there were tears in my eyes. I could barely feel my body at all anymore, and I didn't even know if my hands were still trembling or not.

"We didn't mean to leave you in the dark," Brielle said. "It's just that I was closer by than you were, and this isn't really a conversation to have over text."

"Then why didn't you just pick up the phone and call me, huh?" Phoebe asked me scathingly.

"There's been so much going on…" I started, but Phoebe interrupted me.

"So much going on that you can't even tell one of your best friends…" Phoebe grimaced. "Or should I just say *friends*? You can't pick up the phone to tell her that you've been going through some kind of wild transformation?"

"Did you just demote yourself to friend status?" I asked. "That's not cool at all. You know I care about you so much. Why are you doing this?"

"Why am I doing this?" Phoebe asked. "Why are *you* doing this? You really thought you could just throw all this information at me with Brielle by your side and we'd be all rainbows and sunshine?"

"I don't know what I expected," I said. "But it wasn't this."

"Well, that sure as shit makes two of us, then," Phoebe said. "Because I thought I was driving all the way here to have brunch with my two best friends in the world, and instead I'm met with a stranger and a backstabber."

"Woah." Brielle raised her hands in the air as a sign of peace. "Why don't we slow down for a moment, take a second to breathe? Nobody is a stranger here. We're all still best friends. Kate is just having some issues that she felt the need to share with us. Nothing has to change."

"Whatever," Phoebe said bitingly. "You clearly don't get where I'm coming from at all. I'm exhausted, and this conversation is even more exhausting. I have a long drive home ahead of me."

"So, you're leaving?" I asked. "Just like that?"

Phoebe pushed back her chair and grabbed her jacket. "You've given me a lot to think about. It's safe to say our brunch is officially canceled."

I blinked. I had just lost the person I considered to be the love of my life, and now one of my closest friendships was falling apart. I had no idea how all this had happened so quickly.

"So, I had to hide myself with you, too," I said. "I just didn't know it."

"That's what you do now, isn't it?" Phoebe asked. "You hide things."

Before Brielle and I could get another word in, she turned on her heels and stormed out of the restaurant.

I let out a heavy sigh. "That didn't go exactly as planned."

"It's okay, she just needs time," Brielle said, but she didn't sound confident.

"Let's tell the staff we won't be eating after all," I said. "I think I need to go home and rest. I haven't gotten enough sleep lately. And after this, I definitely need a nap."

"Are you going to be okay on your own?" Brielle asked.

Out of the corner of my eyes, I could see Jer dressed in his familiar gray T-shirt and cargo pants.

"Yeah. I think I'll be okay," I said. "But thanks for checking in."

"Don't let Phoebe's negative reaction make you think everyone is like that." She gave me a hug. "I know what you're going through is awful. And if you want to have a movie night, I'll be so down. And I'll bring all your favorite kinds of ice cream."

"That's going to be a lot of ice cream," I said with a half-smile.

"Well, it's for my best friend in the world, so I have to make sure she's happy." Brielle paused. "You sure you'll be okay?"

"Yeah. I'll take a hot shower and curl up in bed. Maybe read a book."

"Okay." She hugged me one final time. "I'll let you get going."

"Thank you," I said.

I left the restaurant with Jer by my side. I felt reassured by his presence. Once I was out of the restaurant, I let the tears fall. I expressed out loud for just a few moments everything I had kept trapped inside. I had tried so hard to make myself likable to Mike, but I had never thought that I would have to make myself smaller for my friends, too.

"If Phoebe really does care about you, she'll come around," Jer said. "Have faith in that."

*

After my shower, I did as I told Brielle and curled up in bed with a book. I could barely focus on the words. They all blurred together.

I looked over, and Jer was in the bed beside me. He had his hands behind his head, his elbows sticking out on either side.

"Today was a doozy, wasn't it?" he asked.

"Yeah," I said. "It was rough."

It was odd to be sitting in my bedroom, talking to what amounted to an imaginary friend. But he seemed so real, like I could reach out and touch him. He was so detailed it was hard to imagine he wasn't a real person. His black hair was dusted with touches of gray. His cheeks were rosy from smiling at me. Stubble grew on his face.

"I'm glad Veronica didn't show up," I said. "I was expecting her to take the wheel and explode at Phoebe."

"She wanted to," Jer said. He let out a long exhale. "I'm glad she didn't, though. That's a mess we certainly don't need to clean up."

I looked him in the eyes. They were green, with flecks of blue around the edges. They were warm, considerate, compassionate eyes. Eyes that had watched me grow and go through so many changes. Eyes that still looked at me without judgment.

"It's nice to be around you like this," I said. "When it's just you and me. Alone in my room."

"Brings you back, doesn't it?" he asked. "Reminds me of grade school. All those presentations. All those performances. You were so worried about getting up in front of people."

I smiled at him. "But you were there for me. Every time I was scared, or nervous, or thought I was going to fall right off the stage—I'd look up, and there you'd be."

It was hard for me to accept that these two people I had created in my mind had somehow seeped into real life. That my imaginary friend, Jer, and the demon-lady who haunted my dreams, Veronica, were really just pieces of me.

"I was there for therapy, too, you know," Jer said. "When you weren't. When it was Veronica taking control. I was still there, listening. And you know, it's not so strange what you're feeling and thinking. I know it must seem wild to be an adult woman and have an imaginary friend who comforts you."

"It is," I said. "It definitely is. But you know what? At least he's funny."

"And don't forget, incredibly handsome."

I tousled his curls. "Incredibly."

"I mean, if I wasn't, I would have no one but you to blame, now would I?" he asked.

I laughed, despite myself. For a moment, I had almost forgotten about my breakup with Mike and the fight with Phoebe. I had almost forgotten about how broken I felt. That was Jer's magical ability. He could always sense when I needed him most, and he always knew the right things to say.

Veronica walked through the door to the bedroom. She was, for the first time, not dressed to the nines. Her hair was pulled up. She wore a pink sweater and black yoga pants. Her nails were painted a new shade, scintillating blue this time. She sat down on the bed. She seemed quiet, subdued, and I wondered if it had anything to do with my energy levels after today. She didn't have any fight left in her because I had extinguished the fire raging within.

"I'm tired," Veronica said. She yawned, as if to prove a point.

"Me, too," I said. "But I don't want to go to sleep yet. I was having a nice talk with Jer."

"Talk to him in your dreams," she whined. "I'm tired of being conscious. We need a nap. Stat."

"Tough cookies," I said. "We're staying awake."

"I know," Jer said. "Let's vote on it. Raise your hand if you would like to stay awake."

Both Jer and I raised our hands. Veronica stuck out her tongue.

"Fine, whatever," she said. "At least do something *interesting*. Read the book in your hands if you're going to stay awake."

"I think I'd rather stay up and reminisce some more with Jer," I said. "I was just remembering how in high school I had to do this speech in front of the whole school, and I was so worried about it, because I had such bad stage fright. And my peers certainly weren't any help. They laughed the entire rehearsal about how much of an idiot I was."

"Screw those guys," Veronica muttered.

"Yeah, for real," Jer said. "They weren't worth your time."

"But when I went up on stage, I wasn't alone." I smiled. "I knew I had you there with me, Jer. Even if I couldn't see you. How funny to think you started off as a childhood imaginary friend."

"I'm still your friend," he said. "I'm just a bit sturdier now."

"You mean harder to get rid of," Veronica said. "Speaking of, you did try to get rid of us before. Didn't work super well. Wouldn't recommend doing it again."

"I did? When?" I asked.

"The last time you were on medication," Jer said.

"What? I was on medication? When was this? Why don't I remember it?" As the question left my mouth, I knew the answer would be obvious. I had forgotten because I had dissociated. "Surely, I can't have forgotten a whole prescription. I'd have follow-ups with my doctor. It's something I'd have to take every day."

"Yeah, it is," Jer said slowly. "But it's also something that we dealt with for you. Kind of like therapy."

"No way." I launched myself out of bed and rushed to the bathroom. I saw my panic-stricken expression for a moment before I opened the bathroom cabinet. Sitting before me were bottles I didn't recognize, with labels I didn't recognize, but they were all undeniably mine. My name, Kate Moore, was listed on all of them.

I grabbed two bottles and pulled them out. "What even is this?"

"Like I said, they're medications we were taking to try and control the blackouts and things," Jer said.

I pulled my phone out of my pocket and searched up the names of the medications. The two in my hand were antidepressants. The other bottles sitting neatly on the shelf contained antipsychotics.

"So, you see, we've gone down that route before," Jer said. "We've tried medications. We've done everything that Mike suggested doing. It just didn't work for us."

I put the pills back in the cabinet and shut the door. I stared at my reflection. Neither Jer nor Veronica were in the mirror with me. It was disconcerting, so I looked away from my reflection.

"So, he broke up with me for nothing," I said. I was too tired to cry anymore. I had shed all the tears I was capable of shedding. Still, a dry sob racked my frame.

"Oh, come on," Veronica said. "It's not that bad. Now you're one step ahead, right? You know what we've tried. You know what works, and what doesn't."

"Except I don't really," I said. "I don't remember how long I even tried these medications—did I give them enough time to even work?"

"You were on each of them long enough to know they didn't work for you," Jer said. "The side effects were way too damaging. Either you'd be dead asleep all day, or you would barely be able to think. Some of them made your anxiety even worse. It wasn't worth it, in the end, to stay on any of them."

"I wish I had realized this sooner," I said. "If I had known, I could have told Mike."

"Mike wouldn't have understood, even if you were on medication," Jer said. "He wasn't willing to slow down and check in with you."

"He was scared," Veronica added. "I always knew he was a coward."

"That's a low blow," I said. "Mike is a good guy. He just got overwhelmed by all of this."

"Yeah, and broke your heart in the process," Veronica said. "Maybe a 'good guy,' but not a very considerate one."

I paused. "You have a point. He did leave me on read for days."

Jer nodded. "And you agonized over whether or not you would still be together on the other side of this."

"A *considerate* person would have at least spoken to you sooner," Veronica said. "He wouldn't have waited for you to call. He would have called first."

I shuffled back to the bedroom and sat down on the bed. "Maybe Brielle was right. Maybe I shouldn't be alone right now."

"We're here, aren't we?" Jer asked.

"Yeah, you are, but maybe I need…" I stopped myself.

"A *real* friend?" Veronica asked.

"Yeah, I guess so." I winced. "Sorry."

"No worries," Jer said. He patted me on the back. "Do what you have to do to feel better. We'll be here, waiting."

*

Brielle showed up a few hours later. I'd texted her to come over. She had been more than delighted to hear that I had reconsidered her offer. When I opened my apartment door, I found her standing there with three tubs of ice cream held in her arms.

"Surprise!" she said. "I really meant it when I said all of your favorite flavors."

"Chocolate chip cookie dough, cookies and cream, and…is that banana ice cream?" I asked.

"You bet your lucky stars it is!" she said. "Couldn't leave you hanging like that, could I?"

I stepped out of the way, and Brielle made a beeline for the kitchen. She went to put the ice cream away in the freezer.

"Which one do you want first?" she asked.

"Let's start with the cookie dough," I said. "We never decided on a movie, either."

"Depends on what you want to watch," she said. "But I was thinking we could do a classic feel-good movie. Maybe *Pride and Prejudice*?"

"A romance movie? After a breakup? I suspect you just want to see me cry some more," I said.

"I do not!" she exclaimed. "I just want you to let out all of those pent-up emotions you're keeping inside. It might help to have a really good cry."

My eyes were already sore. "I think I've cried enough for the next decade, at least."

"If not a romance movie, then what should we put on?" Brielle asked.

"I was thinking of something more action packed. Violent, even. Something as far from my reality as possible."

"Violence might be a bit much after the heavy day we've had," she said. "What about a comedy?"

"That sounds good. Let's put on something silly."

"I have a YouTube playlist specifically for this purpose! Let me just get it set up. Do you mind if I use your laptop?"

I shook my head. "Go ahead. You have free rein over the entire apartment. What's mine is yours."

"Thanks."

I took out two bowls for the ice cream. Jer and Veronica stood nearby, watching me intently. I had become so accustomed to seeing them in real life that it no longer startled me to look over and see them there. Jer waved. I smiled at him but didn't wave back. I didn't want to scare Brielle, and she didn't need to know that I was hallucinating during our movie night. It would only freak her out.

"Okay, so admittedly, the first few videos are just the funniest scenes from *Firefly* and *Buffy*," Brielle said. "But we love those shows, right? So that'll be sure to cheer you up."

"I'm so down for nostalgia right now," I said. "Take me back to the better days."

"Sit back and relax, because that's where we're going," Brielle said.

We sat down on the couch and threw up our legs on the coffee table. Brielle cast my laptop screen to the TV, and we started on her playlist. We watched dozens of videos. Most had me laughing so hard, it was easy to forget all the troubles the day had brought. I easily lost track of time.

"I hope you know Phoebe will come around eventually," Brielle said, after the last video played. "She was just a bit shocked."

"Did you hear this from her?" I asked. "Seems unusually honest coming from her."

"She didn't tell me exactly," Brielle replied. "I've just known her for a while. So have you. You remember how she gets upset like this and usually comes back a few days later apologetic. She'll come back this time the same way. I bet she'll even send you flowers."

"She can keep her flowers. After the stunt she pulled at the restaurant, I don't think it'll be so easy to make up."

"But if she reaches out, will you accept her apology?"

I snorted. "That's a big if. But yes, if she reaches out, I'll accept her apology."

"Good." Brielle smiled. She looked at the empty bowl in my lap. "Do you want some more ice cream?"

"No, I think the brain freeze is starting to hurt a little."

Brielle laughed. "Then how about some hot chocolate? Isn't that your favorite hot drink?"

"It is. But I think the sugar rush from all the ice cream will be keeping me up tonight."

"What would you like to do now?" she asked.

"I dunno. We can just hang out and chat."

Jer appeared beside me on the couch. It made sense that he

was there, given how stressed I had been today.

"Well, you know how you said you wished you could talk to Jer or Veronica? He's here now."

"Really?" Brielle perked up. "What's he saying?"

I looked at Jer. He smiled. "You can tell her that I'm really glad you have a friend like her," he said. "It's what I've always wanted for you."

"He says he's glad that I have you in my life," I said.

"What about Veronica?" Brielle asked.

"She's quiet right now," I replied. "But let me check."

Jer shot me a warning look. Veronica appeared on the smaller couch opposite us, inspecting her nails.

"I'm in the same boat as Jer here," Veronica said. "I'm glad you have a friend. Beats being alone and crying over ice cream by yourself. At least you're making a social event out of your misery."

I smiled at Brielle, editing Veronica's words. "She's glad you're in my life, too."

"I just wish you'd do something other than watch movies," Veronica said.

"Like what?" I asked. Brielle didn't seem to mind that I was talking to thin air.

"Like playing an instrument. Practice the piano," Veronica said. "There's something you haven't been keeping up with as diligently as usual."

"Because I just went through a breakup," I retorted. "Besides, I don't feel like playing the piano right now."

"Which is exactly why you should do it," Veronica insisted. "Here, let me show you why you should practice."

A shiver passed over me. I felt myself fade. The things in the room seemed less familiar, less mine. They belonged to someone else. Veronica took control. I watched as my body moved.

Veronica sat down at the piano. There was no sheet music, but it wasn't needed. We knew which piece to play. Veronica had been working on it for a decade now, perfecting the performance. "Moonlight Sonata" by Beethoven.

I watched as my fingers floated over the keys, my foot pressing the pedal, my body gliding along with the music. I listened as the music swelled and faded. The heavy, loud tones of the left hand. The melody of the right hand. It filled me, and I felt for the first time in years that I was telling a story with my music. I was not only speaking to the piano, but I was singing along with it, body, spirit, and mind.

When the piece was over, I turned to Brielle and smiled. She was gaping.

"Wow," Brielle said. "That was...amazing."

"Thank you," Veronica said with my voice. I sounded harsher, huskier.

"You've never played the piano for me before," Brielle said. "Did you know that?"

"Probably with good reason," I heard myself say. "Kate rarely practices."

Pride swelled within me, but it wasn't mine. Veronica had spent countless hours perfecting the piece and committing it to memory.

"I'll play more for you some time," Veronica said. "We could definitely use the audience."

"We?" Brielle repeated, then fell silent for a moment. "Oh. Am I speaking with Veronica right now?"

"Yes," Veronica replied.

"I appreciate you showing me your music," Brielle said, rather shyly.

Gone was any of the sadness and grief I had felt over my

breakup with Mike. In its place was appreciation for Brielle. Veronica wanted nothing more than to show our friend how much she meant to us. Her way of doing that was through music. Mine would have probably been through words, or a hug. But that wasn't Veronica's way.

"There's a lot that Kate could improve on," Veronica said. "Practicing her instruments being one of them."

"I've heard your music before, but only ever stuff you've composed digitally," Brielle said. "It really is different to watch you play. You get so into it."

"At least that decade of lessons wasn't for nothing," Veronica replied. "If I had control over the body more often, I would force her to play. But it's not that easy."

"Why don't you have…control more often?" Brielle asked.

We could both hear the hesitancy in her voice. My first instinct would be to comfort her, but Veronica ignored it. Being nervous was just a reasonable side effect of talking to us when we were like this.

"Kate makes it difficult for me to take over," Veronica said. "Jer, too, although right now he is being admittedly chill."

Jer hadn't moved from the couch next to Brielle. He stayed silent, but he was staring at us disapprovingly. Perhaps not as chill as Veronica made him seem.

"Does Jer ever take control?" Brielle asked.

"Not much," Veronica said. "He prefers to sit back and watch from the sidelines. His goals align more with Kate's."

"And yours don't?" Brielle asked.

"I have greater ambitions than Kate does," Veronica said. "I see so much potential in us. We could be so much more than what we are. We could make more music—and make more money. We could go on a tour of the world. Explore. See things for ourselves.

Really find out who we are."

"But Kate would rather stay here," Brielle said. "Is that the issue between you two?"

Veronica laughed shortly. "Only one issue? Darling, there is far more going on here than a fight over who wants to travel where. Although I'll admit, being stuck in this tiny shoebox apartment doesn't help get the creative juices flowing."

"I agree that Kate would benefit from getting out more," Brielle said.

"We all would," Veronica replied. She sighed. "But that's unlikely to happen any time soon."

"It's cool that you have your own dreams and stuff," Brielle said. "I just hope you know that Kate is doing her absolute best."

Veronica sniffed. "I know that. I just think if she tried a little harder, her best would shine even brighter."

"I can agree with that," Brielle said. "But do keep in mind what Mike meant to her…and now that he's gone, she's feeling small. Broken. Fragile. Have you felt that way before?"

There was a flash of anger. A memory burst through my mind. The memory of yelling at my father. I had felt small, broken, and fragile then. And so had Veronica. She was born from feelings like that.

"Of course, I know what it's like," Veronica said. "I've lived the same life Kate has. Sometimes, more of it."

"Then you should be gentle with her," Brielle advised. "You won't make things any better by telling her to pull herself up by the bootstraps. It doesn't work that way. She has a broken heart. She needs tenderness."

"Tenderness is weakness," Veronica said. "If I let her feel weak, then…"

"Then what?" Brielle asked.

"I can't ever let her be weak," Veronica concluded.

"Why not?"

"Because she's already weak enough. And think of what happens when she lets her guard down. People like Mike come into her life, and then I have to put all this effort into undoing her mess. Do you know how much it sucks to sit by and watch her make bad decisions?"

"Is that what you would call Mike?" Brielle asked. "A bad decision?"

"Wouldn't you?" Veronica shot back. "He had no clue that Kate had ever been on medication, to begin with. And they dated for what, a year? How had he not even cared enough to check what medication she was taking?"

"Mike was never really all up in her business," Brielle said.

"More than that, he never seemed to care about what was going on with her," Veronica said. "Period. He used her for her body. He found us to be appealing, physically, and the rest was just details."

"I didn't know Kate had tried medication, though," Brielle said. "Does that make me a bad friend?"

"No," Veronica replied immediately. Guilt lingered in our chest. "You're not a bad friend. You're one of the best friends we've ever had. You've been by our side through so much. Since high school. That's a long time to know someone."

"And I've watched you grow and change into this incredible person." Brielle motioned to me. "You're complex. Beyond even my understanding."

"Then you know you're a good friend," Veronica said. "The issue isn't that Mike didn't know about the medication. We didn't tell him about that. I did my best to hide it from Kate, and I did it well. Whenever we'd take the medication, we'd dissociate, and that would be my chance. I was her blind spot for years."

"Then what's your real issue with Mike?" Brielle asked.

"He's just not good enough for me," I said.

My vision corrected itself. Warmth returned to my limbs. The chair, the piano, the couches, even the coffee table—I remembered it all as belonging to me. It no longer seemed unfamiliar.

"I'm so sorry about that," I said. My head was spinning. I felt like I needed to lie down. I slumped over.

"It's okay." Brielle rushed over to my side. "Can I get you anything?"

"No, no," I said. "Thank you so much for coming over tonight. I'm *so* beat. I've never had a conversation like that before, with Veronica taking control and being...there for it all."

"Yeah, that was definitely a surreal experience," Brielle said. "But you're sure you're okay? There's nothing I can get you?"

"Nope." I cleared my throat. "I'm fine, really. I probably just need more rest. It was kind of you to come over and spend the evening with me."

"Of course." Brielle went to hug me, but I stepped back.

"Ah, sorry." I motioned to myself. "I'm so sweaty right now. I think it's the adrenaline wearing off."

"All right, I'll head home. Thanks for having me over. And feel free to text me if you wake up freaking out or anything. I know how bad your anxiety can get after a breakup."

"Thank you," I said. "Will do."

I was hopeful that I wouldn't have to text her in the middle of the night because of nightmares or bad memories of Mike. I had done that a lot in my early twenties, when I was dating, but things were different now. *I* was different now. Not only did I know about Jer and Veronica's existence, but I had managed to communicate with them. We were all working together now to keep our ship afloat.

Brielle looked like she wanted to hug me again but thought better of it. "I'll talk to you soon, 'kay?"

"Yeah," I said. "Talk soon."

Jer and Veronica vanished. It was just me and my feelings. And those feelings weren't great. Anguish, guilt, and remorse. I felt bad that Mike had left me and I couldn't call him over and ask him to spend the night. I felt bad that Phoebe hadn't texted me to say she was sorry after blowing up at the restaurant. And I felt bad for myself, for every time I had dissociated recently and not quite acted like myself.

Outside of my work, who was I really? Was Veronica right? Did we really need to travel the world to find out who we were? Or could the answers be found here, in Vancouver, with Naomi working by my side?

I went to sleep with a head full of unanswered questions and troubled thoughts.

Chapter Five

November 2022

I wanted to know who Kate Moore really was. I wanted to feel like I was whole, instead of in pieces.

My reflection hadn't felt like me since the day Mike found me lying on the kitchen floor. Maybe even before then.

I experimented with makeup. I did a full glam look, as though I were preparing for a photoshoot. I put on heavy eyeshadow and eyeliner, lipstick, blush, and contour. The more makeup I applied, the more I found I looked like Veronica. Mission failed.

I wiped it all off with a washcloth. I started again with a blank canvas. Without makeup, my features seemed more masculine. I could see hints of Jer in the shape of my jaw. In the heaviness of my brow. In the shadows under my eyes. In the smile lines around my mouth.

But which part was Kate? All of it? Or none of it? I inspected my eyes again. Green. These were my eyes. Why didn't they feel like mine? They had witnessed my entire life. Even the pieces I was missing. I wished I could open my head like a hard drive and see all the things I had forgotten.

Staring at my reflection wasn't helping me, and neither was applying makeup. I stepped away from the mirror and turned off the bathroom light. I preferred the dark. There were no reflective surfaces in the dark. I couldn't see how wrong I looked.

"This isn't healthy, you know," Veronica said.

I sat down against the wall and curled up into a ball. "Thanks, genius. As if I couldn't figure that one out myself."

"You don't have to work so hard to try and 'find yourself' in the mirror. You're not going to like what you see."

I groaned. "How do you know that?"

"Because you're looking out when you should be looking inward," she replied.

"Jeez, what kind of philosophy major bullshit is that?"

"It's true. None of us see ourselves in this body. How can we when we all look so different?"

"I'm just looking for some stability in this. An anchor. Something to hold on to."

"Well, sorry to tell you, but your pretty little face isn't it."

"Then what is?" I asked. "Because I keep looking and looking, and I just feel like there are pieces of me that are...lost."

Jer appeared by my side. He wrapped an arm around my shoulders. "It won't feel that way forever. We're going to help you put the pieces together."

I smiled. "Thank you. There must be a way for me to feel some sense of myself, though, right?"

"Maybe through your music?" Jer suggested. "You might

connect to something you've created."

"I've tried that," I admitted. "I've listened to some of my earlier improv performances. None of it resonated with me. I tried to listen to my pop stuff. Rock stuff. None of it felt like me. In fact, I barely remember writing the music at all. Some of it seems totally new. But still not me."

"New. That's an idea." Jer smiled. "Why don't you try writing something new?"

"Like what?" I asked. "I don't even know which genre I want to work with."

"Why don't you get your violin?" Jer asked. "It's been a while since you played. Maybe it'll help to calm you down. That always used to do the trick, when you were younger."

I sighed. "I haven't properly played in a while. I recorded a sample for a track I was working on, but that barely counts. It wasn't really a full piece."

"Playing music for work isn't the same as writing music for fun," Jer said.

I got up, went to my room, and pulled out my violin case from under my bed. I popped open the latches and pulled out the instrument. I applied resin to the bow, breathing in the familiar amber scent. When I placed the violin on my shoulder, it felt natural. Like an extension of myself.

I started playing slowly and softly. I thought of Brielle. Of how she protected me, kept me safe. Of how she hugged me or placed her hand on mine. The music swelled. My bowing grew faster. I thought of how anxious I was to let go of what I had with Mike. Of how I had lost him, because I didn't fit into his neat little narrative of what counted as healthy. And I thought of Brielle being there to comfort me. Her arms open wide and inviting.

I was looking for an anchor in a safe harbor, and I couldn't find it within myself. But I found it there, with my friend. I slowed down the pace of the music, quieted the tone. Calm washed over me. I finished the song with a long, low note. I let the silence fill my ears afterward, my body tingling with sensation from the vibrations of the violin. I realized something. I had feelings for Brielle.

"That was beautiful," Jer said. "More than beautiful, that was *you*."

"But these feelings…" My breath came in quick bursts.

"Take a deep breath," Jer instructed me. "It'll be okay."

"No, it won't!" I exclaimed. "I had no idea that I even had a crush on Brielle. Now it's all I can think about! Since when has this even been going on?"

"Veronica has liked her for a while. We just thought it best to keep who liked who separated. You liked Mike, and she liked Brielle. But you know, since you have control of the body, we thought it was best to let you have it your way."

"And because she's my best friend!" I exclaimed. "I still can't get over that. I would never… I could never ruin our friendship like that."

"Oh, please," Veronica said. "She clearly likes you back. It's been years of this 'will they, won't they,' and now that you're finally single again, you can explore it."

"I don't want to explore it!" I snapped.

"You sure about that?" Veronica asked. "Methinks the lady doth protest too much. Don't you agree, Jer?"

Jer threw up his hands. "This is entirely up to Kate. I'm not getting mixed up in this."

"Brielle would think the idea is ridiculous," I said.

"I think you know what I'm about to say," Veronica replied.

"You're about to dare me to ask her." I crossed my arms in

front of my chest. "No way. I've had a hard enough day as it is. I do not need to make things more complicated with my best friend."

"If you won't..." Veronica started, letting her words trail off ominously.

Then I will.

For the second time that night, Veronica took control of me. She grabbed my phone, and before I could stop her, she had written a text message to Brielle.

> **Me:** *I think you should know that I have feelings for you.*

I stared at the text. My entire body shook with the effort to not send it.

"This isn't right," I said through clenched teeth. "If we're really going to tell her how we feel, then it should be done properly. In person."

You're stalling, I heard Veronica say in my mind. *Just send the text and get it over with.*

"No!" I exclaimed. "I don't want to. This is all happening way too fast. It's not fair to me at all."

Oh, and you dating Mike for a full year was fair to us? Veronica's voice boomed in my mind. *Just send the text, please.*

Despite everything inside me screaming not to do it, I sent the message.

I watched as Brielle opened the message and read it. "Seen." She typed, then stopped. The three dots appeared again on my screen, then vanished. It was agonizing.

"No matter what she says, she's still your best friend," Jer said. "Think of it as just being a bit more honest with both yourself and her."

"This is still so new to me," I whispered. "And I didn't want it to happen like this."

"If I didn't do it now, you would never have done it," Veronica said. She was sitting stiffly now at the piano. "You'll thank me later."

"Somehow I doubt that," I ground out.

> **Brielle:** *Hey. You sure you're okay? Doesn't sound like you.*

I breathed a sigh of relief. Of course, Brielle would be able to tell when it was me talking and when it wasn't. Even over text. A huge wave of appreciation washed over me at the thought.

> **Me:** *Ignore me. I'm having a rough night. Dissociation is bad.*

> **Brielle:** *That's what I thought. Don't worry. I won't judge you for what you say right now :)*

I put down my phone.
"So, what are you going to do about it?" Veronica asked.
"I have no idea," I said. "Lots of journaling? More music?"
"A little journaling probably wouldn't hurt," Jer replied.
"And some sleep," Veronica said, with a big yawn.
I agreed with Veronica. I needed to get some rest. I headed to bed.

*

When I woke up, it was past midnight. The only light was from my TV, a red dot that seemed like a laser shooting through my eyes. The sheets clung to me. I was scared. My arms and legs ached as if I had been running. My throat was sore as though I had been yelling. I threw the blanket over my head. I always felt safe under my covers.

I wished Brielle was beside me. I grabbed my pillow and pulled it under the blankets with me. My breath came out in ragged bursts. Nightmares. Brielle was right—I was going through the same cycle I went through every breakup. Waking up panicking and alone at night, my skin lined with sweat.

The same thought kept repeating over and over in my head: *I'm scared, I'm scared, I'm scared.*

"Do you think they're going to come get us?" a small voice whispered.

I looked around. Veronica and Jer weren't there with me. I felt disoriented, on top of fearful.

"I don't want them to get me," the voice said again.

In front of me appeared a child, no more than eleven years old. She hugged a familiar cat teddy to her chest. My old cat teddy that I had named Bow. She looked like me. I could see the similarities immediately. Her dark hair, cut into bangs the same way I'd it done when I was little. But her hair was shorter than mine had been. I also didn't recognize the dragon pajamas she wore.

"Nobody's going to get you," I said slowly, realizing what was happening. I was hallucinating again. And this time it was someone new. "I've never met you before. Can I ask who you are?"

"I'm scared." The girl moved further into the blanket, away from me.

"It's okay, I won't hurt you," I assured her. "You can trust me."

"My name is Mila," she said.

"Hi, Mila," I replied. "I'm Kate."

"I know," she shot back. "But will those bad guys be coming to get us?"

"Bad guys? You mean from the nightmares?"

Mila nodded. She clutched Bow closer to her chest. "Will they be coming? Is that why you are hiding?"

"No bad men are coming to get us. We're going to be all right."

"You sure?" she asked. "It seemed so real."

"It's not real, I promise. It was just a bad dream."

"And the other Bad Man?" Mila asked. "You wanted him to be here. You were wishing he was here to keep us safe from the bad men in your dreams."

"Mike?" I shook my head. "You don't have to worry about him. He's not coming to get us, either. We're safe under here."

I didn't know how to comfort her. This was our first time having a real conversation, even though I was sure I had sensed her in my mind before. I thought of what comforted me in moments like these and pulled inspiration from Jer. I reached out and patted Mila's hand gently.

"It's just you and me right now," I said.

Mila relaxed her grip on her teddy. A small smile appeared on her lips. "I'm glad to have a sister like you."

I had never thought of my personalities as siblings, but the comparison made sense. If they truly were individuals, then they were closer to me than friends. They knew me more intimately. They were family—perhaps not one I had chosen, but one I had made for myself when I had found my own family lacking.

"Come here," I said. Mila inched forward. I wrapped my arms around her and pulled her to my chest. "I know things have been hard lately. But I'm going to do everything I can to keep you safe, okay?"

"Okay." I could feel her shoulders relax under my arm. "Will we be seeing Jer today?"

"I hope so. How do you know Jer?"

"We're family, duh," she said, as though I should have known better. "Of course I know him. He's my big brother."

The fear that had gripped me from the nightmares was slowly dissipating. Instead, I grew intensely curious. I wanted to talk to her more, but Mila's presence faded as I became calmer.

"Don't go yet," I said softly. "I want to get to know you better."

But she was slipping away, and soon it was just me under the covers. I threw the blanket off my head, acutely aware of how damp my sheets were from sweat. I stripped the bed and threw my sheets into the wash. I didn't care that it was nearly 2:00 a.m. I wanted fresh sheets, and I only had one set. I sat down on a stool next to the washer while I waited for the cycle to end.

I wished Mila had stayed for longer. I didn't know that one of my personalities was a child. For the first time, the intense fear I felt made sense. I was carrying a lot of that fear in Mila from when I was young.

"You did well, you know," Jer said, appearing by my side. "For the first meeting, you did a great job."

"Do you think so?" I asked.

"Totally."

I wasn't surprised anymore when Jer made sudden appearances. If I focused, I could tell when it was about to happen. I could feel a tug on my consciousness, as though someone were tapping me on the shoulder gently, then he would appear.

"Have I ever dissociated into Mila?" I asked. "I know I've dissociated before and been Veronica. But never you. Is it the same with her?"

"It's hard to say," Jer said. "Mila doesn't take control the same way Veronica does. But sometimes you'll share a consciousness.

You'll both be 'at the front,' so to speak. Fronting, as Naomi calls it. When Mila is at the front with you, you become more like her."

"And what does it mean to be like her?" I asked.

"How did it feel in the moment?" Jer asked.

"I felt scared," I admitted. "Terrified, even, of things that weren't real. And things that were."

"When Mila is fronting, you can become more anxious. But there are also good things about her fronting with you. You're gentler with yourself. You take extra care. And I think that's really needed now, of all times. I think Mila showed up because you needed her."

"It's probably been a while since I've needed a kid to help me out with my nightmares," I half-joked.

"She hasn't been around as much as the rest of us, it's true," Jer said. "But that's partly because she's been so scared of everything going on."

"So how do I get in touch with her?" I asked. "Writing? Playing music?"

"Those are good ideas. But think smaller. What are things you enjoyed when you were a child?"

"I liked playing Pokémon games and collecting stuffed animals."

"Then try doing more of that. I think if you bond over emotional things, you'll find a way to connect with Mila. Find a way to make her comfortable."

"Is she not comfortable now?"

Jer raised a brow. "That should be obvious, shouldn't it? If she's so terrified, there's hardly any time for her to relax and have fun. And God knows, we all need a bit of that right now."

"Is that how she helps me? Helps all of us? By reminding us to have fun?"

"That's part of it. Her presence in your life isn't as straightforward as mine or Veronica's. You'll have to put in the effort to establish a relationship with her."

"Well, it'll be another hour before the sheets are done drying," I said. "Maybe I should play a video game."

Jer smiled. "Sounds like a good idea to me."

"Hey, would you mind sticking around? Something tells me Mila would be happy to see you, too."

"Sure. There's nowhere else I'd rather be."

I went to the living room and opened my organizational drawer. I pulled out my Nintendo Switch and its case. I popped in the most recent Pokémon game and sat on the couch. I was delighted at the nostalgic music and the bright colors.

"My favorite Pokémon is Eevee," Mila said, appearing to my right. "Because Eevee can evolve into many different things."

"Is that so?" I asked, trying to contain my excitement at seeing her again. I didn't want to scare her away like I had earlier.

"Yeah," she said. "Who's your favorite Pokémon?"

"My favorite is Charizard," I said. "Because I've always loved dragons."

"Me, too!" Mila's face brightened. She pointed at her pajamas. "I even have them on right now! That's how much I love them."

"Wow, you really do like dragons!" I exclaimed, trying to match her energy.

She nodded vigorously. "I do, I do. Did you know that there are other dragon Pokémon?"

I smiled at her enthusiasm. "Really? Tell me about it."

Mila grabbed the Switch from me and started playing, prattling on about her favorite monsters in the game. Her eyes were bright and round, and she spoke a mile a minute.

"Hey," Jer said, from my left side. "You're not even going to say hello to your big brother?"

Mila stopped speaking abruptly and smiled at him. "Hi."

"Hi there," he said. "You're telling Kate about your favorite Pokémon?"

"Yeah!" Mila beamed. "Kate likes the same things as me."

"Well, of course she does. Kate is your big sister after all," Jer said. "Who do you think got you to play all those games to begin with? She did."

"*Wow*," Mila exaggerated the word. "That's so cool. Thank you, Kate!"

"You're welcome," I said.

I had never spent much time around kids. I never had to babysit much growing up, and I didn't have any younger siblings. I had no idea what to say to Mila. I wasn't sure how to speak with her. On the one hand, she seemed very bright and intelligent. On the other hand, she was so small and cute in her dragon pajamas I wasn't sure if a serious conversation would fly over her head or not.

"I'm glad I got to meet you tonight," I said. "And that we could talk again, under happier circumstances."

"Me, too," Mila said. "And I got to see Jer-Bear!"

Jer got up from his seat and walked over to Mila. He gave her a great big hug, lifting her up from where she sat, and she giggled. I laughed, too, almost in the same tone. I was surprised at the freeness I felt inside my chest when I laughed like that. I was really happy in a way I hadn't been since my younger years.

Jer was right. Connecting with Mila really was important.

"Is it almost bedtime?" Mila asked. She stuck out her tongue. "I don't want to go to bed again."

"The sheets will be done drying in a bit and then we'll go back to sleep," I said.

"I don't want to!" Mila sounded anxious. Fear shot through me. I was feeling what she was feeling, and it wasn't good. "I don't want the Bad Men to get us again!"

"Nobody will get you," Jer said. "That was a bad dream, remember? You're safe now."

"Is there anything I can do to make going to bed easier?" I asked.

"Don't have stupid nightmares," Mila muttered.

"Okay, I'll do my best. And what else?"

"Hide that laser pointer," she replied. She meant the TV. I picked up a baggy shirt and covered the television and its bright light.

"Done," I said. "Anything else?"

"Don't call Mike," she said. "I don't want to talk to him."

"Okay, I promise, I won't call Mike. Would it help if I kept a lamp on, so that when we woke up, we could see the room? Just in case we have nightmares. I don't want to hide under the covers again. What do you say?"

"Yeah," Mila said slowly. "Let's do that."

Once the clean sheets were replaced, I carried a half-awake Mila over to the bed. I put her gently into the bed and brought the covers up to her face. She smiled at me sleepily.

"Thanks," she mumbled. "I loved playing with you. Let's do it again soon."

"Okay." I smiled. "Sounds good."

It wasn't long before I curled up in the space beside where I had left her and drifted off to sleep.

*

I woke up a second time with a gasp. The lamp was on. It wasn't as distressing to wake up to a lit room, rather than darkness. I was glad I had thought ahead. The nightmares had been bad again. Bad enough that the sheets I had just washed were soaked with sweat once more. I had dreamed of two gunmen chasing me through my building, and of jumping out of a window to try to flee. I had even imagined falling, and the adrenaline still coursed through my veins.

I stayed awake for the rest of the night, not wanting to have any further nightmares. I figured that staying awake was the best way to stave them off. If I didn't sleep, I wouldn't have bad dreams. The hours flew by. Light filtering through my window signaled morning time.

I wasn't ready to get out of bed. I had a desire to punish myself, the way I used to. I had the scars on my legs to remind me of darker times, when I would cut. These days I had avoided doing anything like it—but that didn't mean I didn't still get the urges. Especially when I was feeling ashamed. And I was ashamed that Mike had left me. He hadn't broken up with me because we were deeply incompatible. It hadn't been because he wanted kids, and I didn't. We hadn't even gotten to that topic yet. And it wasn't because I wanted marriage, and he didn't. We had only been together one year. We weren't thinking about any of those things. But despite the year we shared together, he had left me. All because I was dealing with my health the way I felt was best.

Rationally, I knew that his decision was beyond my control. Emotionally, I couldn't help but feel it was my fault. That if I had been better at handling things, maybe he would still be here. I felt like everything bad that had happened was on me. It was my responsibility. And I had failed. I had failed at the relationship I had tried so hard to keep.

Being with Mike hadn't always been easy. The year we had been together had felt like four. We argued often. Over trivial things, like why I hadn't called him one evening. He could be a bit controlling that way—he always wanted my attention when *he* wanted it and otherwise would cast me to the wayside. But I was meant to be available whenever he wanted to talk to me.

Mila appeared next to me. "I thought I told you to stop having those stupid nightmares."

"I'm sorry," I said, startled by her appearance. "I tried to stay calm, but that meant staying awake."

Mila frowned. "You're still thinking about the Bad Man."

I sat up in bed. "He's not so bad, you know."

"No, he only broke your heart," I heard Veronica say. She stood by the door. "There are things about Mike I know you'd rather forget, but it's not always that easy."

"Please, do we have to air out my dirty laundry in front of her?" I asked, motioning to Mila.

"She sees everything we see," Veronica shot back. "She doesn't need to be censored."

"I just stop watching when I don't like something," Mila said matter-of-factly.

"Why are you both here?" I asked. "I thought I was going to be alone all night."

"You were, technically," Veronica said. "It's 7:00 a.m. And I'm here because you need help with the Mike situation. Don't ask me why the kid is here, though."

"Because I want to be," Mila said simply.

"Look, you can't beat yourself up over this Mike thing," Veronica said. "He took you for granted for the year you were together. You know that most of your fights weren't your fault but were because he was trying to control your every move. He even got you to change your hair dye!"

"He said that the jet black didn't suit me," I said. "And he was right. He was just being honest."

Veronica snorted. "There's a difference between being honest and just being rude. He was the latter."

I picked up the spare pillow and buried my face in it. "I'm going to have to tell my mom we broke up."

"Yes, you will," Veronica said. "And she'll probably be disappointed."

"As if I didn't already know that."

"Veronica's being mean!" Mila exclaimed.

"I'm not being mean, I'm telling it like it is," Veronica replied. "And we all know how Mom is going to react."

"Do you want to take over for this one?" I asked. "Do the phone call for me?"

"What do I look like, a personal assistant?" Veronica sneered. "No way. You do the call yourself. I've done enough work for you lately."

"Fine," I said. "I'll do it."

Mom was an early riser. The last time we spoke, it had been a brief catch-up over the phone. Our conversations tended to remain on the short end of things. Mom was always really busy. But I knew she'd have time for this.

I pulled up her contact info and pressed call.

"Kate?" Mom said when she answered the phone. "Is everything all right, honey?"

"Hey, Mom," I said. "Well, that's why I'm calling. Things haven't been great lately."

"You usually text. So, when I saw you calling, I knew it had to be something serious. What happened?"

"Nothing serious." I took a breath. "I just thought I should let you know that Mike and I broke up."

"No!" she exclaimed. "That's horrible. What happened? You two were so great together."

"I've been going through some things with my health lately, and he just didn't believe I was taking care of myself properly."

"And are you?" Mom asked.

"I think I'm doing an okay job." I tried not to get defensive. "I think he just got overwhelmed by all my problems."

"Maybe you put too much on him. You know how men can be. You stress them out too much, and they take off."

"I didn't mean to put too much on his shoulders. I was just trying to share my life with him."

"Oh, honey." Mom sighed. "Maybe your life is a little too much to share."

I hadn't even told her about my mental health concerns, and she already thought I was "too much." I was terrified to think of what she'd say if I let her know I had been hallucinating. She would likely tell me that I'd be alone forever.

"You're right," I said. "Maybe I am a bit too much."

"But that's something you can work on." Mom tried to sound encouraging and upbeat. "You can turn your life around. Start fresh. This is a great opportunity for you. You know what they say: when one door closes, another opens. You'll meet the right guy for you."

"Thanks, Mom."

"I've got to get going now. I'll text you later, okay?"

"Okay. Love you."

"Love you, too."

I threw my phone aside.

"Why did I bother calling?" I asked. "I knew she'd make me feel worse about it."

"She'd have to find out sooner than later," Veronica said. "Or else you'd have to deal with her asking about Mike the next time you went for lunch or something. And that wouldn't be ideal, now, would it?"

"No, it wouldn't," I muttered. "But I'm still not impressed."

"Breakups are hard," Mila said. "You get sad for a long time."

"She's right," Veronica said. "It does take you a while to get over things."

"Where's Jer?" I asked. "I feel like he'd usually be here by now to help me out."

"I'm here," he said, appearing next to Veronica by the door. "What do you need?"

"Nothing, it's just nice to have everyone together in one room," I replied. "I was hoping once I got everyone together, I could fill in some blanks."

"I think it's about time we told her about the box," Jer said.

"No," Veronica replied immediately. "It's too early for her to have access to all that."

"Too late," I said. "You've already mentioned it. What are you guys hiding from me now?"

"There's a box you keep hidden in your closet," Jer said. "There are some books in there that you might find helpful."

I ran over to the closet. I tore through my clothes. I found the box nestled underneath a pile of dresses I had planned to fold and put away for the summer. I took out the box and opened it. The box was full of notebooks. There were big ones and small ones that fit inside pockets. They were full, cover to cover, with writing in blue ink. I flipped through the pages and stopped on an entry.

January 16th, 2021

It's been a long day. Had a fight with Mike. Had to take over, since Kate wasn't able to do it herself. Mike was yelling at me about the state of my room. I always clean before he comes over, but he always finds something to complain about. Today he seemed annoyed that the dishes weren't done when he arrived. I had polished the whole place, except for that one small detail. I don't know why Kate demands he stay in our life. I would much prefer to date someone like Brielle. She's far more understanding, patient, and overall wonderful. Mike does nothing but complain and take up space.

I put down the notebook.

"So these are diary entries from when Veronica was fronting," I said. "I don't even remember this fight with Mike."

"That's why I wrote it down," Veronica said. "I knew you'd forget, or at least, you wouldn't remember what happened while I had control. I knew you'd want to fill in the blanks eventually."

I motioned to the notebook. "Why didn't you want me to see this?"

"Because there's so much information in there, you probably aren't ready for it." Veronica motioned to the bed, where Mila had been. "See? The kid's gone. She usually only leaves when things start to get messy."

"She doesn't like Mike," I observed. "The passage I read mentioned him. She probably wanted to get away because of that. But why?"

"It's all in there," Jer said, motioning to the books. "All of the memories you're missing. Or at least, most of them. We tried to journal as much as possible so we wouldn't lose things."

"How far back do these go?" I asked. I picked up another notebook and opened it to a random page.

March 4th, 2012

Passed the French test today. I was worried I'd do poorly, but I did okay. It was easier than expected. Kate hadn't studied much, but that didn't mean I couldn't get a bunch done the night before. Cramming is my specialty. Kate just can't deal with the stress of writing tests. She runs to the bathroom twelve times before the teacher even tells us to start writing. It's an issue. The teacher thought I seemed a little off afterward, though. It's hard to stay Veronica when everyone sees Kate. Miss Keating asked if she could speak to me about some kind of after-school activity, and it took everything in me not to tell her off. I hate that teacher. She is SO boring. I had to smile, the way Kate would, and say "Sure, that sounds great!" in Kate's voice. At least afterward I could go to lunch with Bri.

I gaped. "This goes all the way back to high school. How many of these are there?"

"There's at least a dozen in front of you," Jer said. "More hidden elsewhere or destroyed."

"Let me guess, Veronica burned the ones she didn't want me to read," I said.

"I was *protecting* you," Veronica said. "There are some things you just can't handle, and I stepped in to make sure you were okay."

"Like what? Writing my French test?" I asked. "I can't believe how much you've done for me over the years. How much of my life you've lived."

"How else do you think you got through all of this?" Veronica asked.

I separated the notebooks by the years noted in the diary entries. There were four from high school, six from undergrad and my early twenties, and a few from more recent years. The old notebooks I barely recognized. One of them was blue with gold trim. The other three were from the same set, all blue with different swirling designs on the cover. The recent notebooks were of different shapes and sizes. One had JOURNAL written across the front. Another had an inspirational quote: "This notebook is owned by a BADASS WOMAN." Seemed like stocking stuffers I had gotten for Christmas, or little gifts I had been given for writing music.

"Are there any entries here written by Mila?" I asked.

"Moreso in the earlier journals," Jer said. "As you got older, Mila didn't get to the front as much. For obvious reasons. We couldn't have you dissociating into a child persona while you were at school or work."

I opened an old journal and flipped through it. I paused on a page where the writing looked shakier and the script was different, less refined. I mostly wrote in cursive, but I had broken the trend here.

September 8th, 2009

School sucked today. Boring. At least I got to play a bit today. I cried on the bus today. Because of what Dad said. He told me I stank. Said he could smell me from where he was standing by the door. Which isn't true. I smelled fine. But he told me the others would know how much I stank, and they wouldn't play with me. Well, he was wrong. I had plenty of friends at lunch to play with. Although everyone preferred to talk about boys. Ugh.

"That's an entry written by Mila," I said. "Seems she never really liked dating or talking about boys at all."

"Not her favorite topic, no," Jer said.

I picked up a more recent journal. It was plain burgundy, with a clasp. I flipped through the pages, looking for the shaky handwriting. I found an entry from a year ago.

October 4th, 2021

Mike never wants to play. He never wants to watch TV with me. He's always on the phone. He says it's for work, but I know it's not. And he yells. So much. Reminds me of Dad. He's miserable with us. He is only happy when Kate is there, but she's gone so much these days. So, he is angry. I just hope he keeps his hands to himself. That's what Nana always said, right? We keep our hands to ourselves.

"What did she mean by that?" I asked. "I wish she were here so I could ask her myself."

"It's better that she's not," Jer said. "Mila has a hard time with these memories. She would probably be a sobbing mess if she were here."

"Damn," I said. "Something really bothered her that badly, huh?"

Jer shrugged. "Mike didn't keep his hands to himself."

I felt like he had just dunked my head in ice-cold water. "Was he abusive? How do I not remember this?" I asked. I was cold and numb. Normally, I'd be crying. But I felt cut off from my emotions. I was a detective now, putting together the facts and trying to make sense of it all.

"There are some memories each of us carry," Jer explained. "Your biggest fight with Mike is one you'd prefer to forget."

"Did I write it down?" I asked, searching the pages nervously.

"If you did, it won't be in there anymore," Jer said. "These notebooks can help you fill in some blanks, but…"

I landed on a torn page. "Veronica."

"It wasn't something safe for you to read," Veronica said.

"Since when do you care about what's safe for me, all of a sudden?" I asked.

"I've *always* cared," she retorted. "Just because you don't appreciate the things I do for you doesn't mean I don't care."

"I need to tell Naomi about this," I said. "Too much has happened. I need a therapy session."

"Good thing I already booked one for you," Veronica said. "Check your texts. You should have a session scheduled for Thursday."

She was right. My phone's calendar even had the event included on Thursday afternoon.

"Thanks for booking that," I said, figuring a little appreciation might take me far.

Veronica sniffed. "You're welcome. Just don't make a habit out of it. You book your next session."

"Got it," I said. "And I don't think I'll be going to therapy alone."

"What do you mean?" Jer asked.

"I mention in these journals that Mike didn't keep his hands to himself," I said. "I want to find out what Mila meant by that. I want to explore the things I forgot. Naomi likely has notes on all of this stuff. I want to hear what she has to say. But more than that, I want to hear what Mike has to say."

"You're still considering giving him the time of day after everything that's happened?" Veronica asked.

"I'm not going to take him back," I said. "But doing a therapy session together might be helpful. Hearing his side of the story might help me put the pieces together."

"If you think it will help, then I support you," Jer said.

I picked up my phone and called Mike.

"Hello?" he said.

"Hey," I replied. I tried to keep my voice steady. "I know we haven't really been speaking since things ended. And I know we probably both need space, but...there was something I hope you could do for me. For my health."

"What is it?" he asked apprehensively.

"Would you go to therapy with me?" I asked.

"Like a couple's counseling session?"

"I was thinking it would just be a normal session, but one you could be there for," I said.

"You know what I think about your therapist. She's not a real one. You need a real one."

"Turns out I *have* seen a real doctor about it, and I still preferred Naomi," I said. "Could you please see past your judgments of her for a moment and think about how this could help me?"

"If I go, will I be able to voice how unethical I think her practice is?"

"You can say whatever you want, if you'll just come. I want you there. I think it will be helpful. I think I can remember more when you're around."

"If you think it'll help, sure. I have some PTO I can take. When's your appointment?"

"Thursday afternoon," I said.

"Text me the details," Mike said. "I'll be there."

*

Naomi and I sat in her living room waiting for Mike two days later.

He was ten minutes late. I wasn't entirely surprised—he had been reluctant to come to the session at all. I think the only reason he agreed to show up was to tell the therapist what he thought of her. When he arrived, he didn't apologize or even say hello to either of us. He threw himself on the couch next to me and crossed his arms.

"Thank you for joining us, Mike," Naomi said when he was settled. "Kate told me you'd be coming."

"I'm here," he said. "Let's just get this thing started."

"Kate, I think you wanted to start the session by explaining why you're both here, right?" Naomi asked.

"Yes," I said. "I wanted us both to be here because we've been through a breakup recently and it was about my mental health."

Mike sighed. "If things could change with Kate, I might reconsider."

"What would have to change for you to want to be back in a relationship with her?" Naomi asked.

"She'd have to stop seeing you, for one," Mike said. "I'm sure you've done some real good work psychoanalyzing her, but I don't believe you're the person who's going to help her."

"And why not?" Naomi asked, her face a serene mask.

"Because you don't have the credentials," Mike said bluntly. "You're not even a real therapist yet."

"Have you ever considered that I've been to see real therapists, and they didn't help?" I asked. "Naomi has been helping me, and that's more I can say for the doctors who thought throwing medication at me would make me all better."

"And that's another thing, medication," Mike said. "Did you know that Kate hallucinates? I mean, come on! Something's gotta give here. She can't be wandering around having psychotic episodes."

"And why not?" Naomi asked. "Has she caused harm to herself or to others?"

"Not that I know of." Mike glanced at me quickly. "But she very well *could* hurt herself if she was out there seeing people and things that aren't real."

"Some people live with psychosis and choose not to be medicated," Naomi said. "Kate hasn't done anything wrong."

"I found her on the kitchen floor!" Mike exclaimed. "She was drenched from the rain."

"But she was at home, and she was safe, wasn't she?" Naomi asked.

"She was in distress!" he said. "How can you be so calm about this? It's concerning."

"I can see why that would be concerning for you," Naomi said. "Finding your partner after a dissociative episode would be scary. But Kate was there to explain it to you, and now I'm here to make the rest make sense."

"What I want you to do is to admit that Kate needs help that goes beyond what you can offer," Mike said. A vein pulsed in his forehead. "She's not going to get better coming here and talking about her feelings."

"But I *have* gotten better," I said. "Mike, what you have to realize is that this has been going on my entire life. I've handled it just fine until...well, until recently. But I've found ways to make it work. Ways to trick my brain into handling all those distressing things. What you saw was just a preview into what it's like to live my life right now."

"Why do you think you've handled it fine until recently?" Naomi asked.

"Because until recently, I had managed to keep it away from Mike," I said.

Mike's face reddened. "I'm not some child who needs things to be kept away from me. I could have dealt with all of this."

"Could you?" I shot back. "Because as soon as things started to get bad, you left."

He threw his hands up. "I'm here to try and make it work. Don't attack me."

"Kate, do you think keeping your mental health issues separate from your relationship helped it?" Naomi asked.

"I think it was the right thing to do," I said, sensing Veronica at the edge of my mind. "He didn't handle it all that well when he found out about what I'd been going through. But then again, neither did I. I didn't even have a name for what I was experiencing until recently. It's all so new."

"Mike, could you see yourself finding a way to forge a path forward with Kate, knowing what you know now about her illness?" Naomi asked.

"I don't know," Mike said. "I wish I could say yes, that I'm definitely sure we can make this work. But knowing that it's something you've been dealing with this long—that when I met you, Kate, you had all of this going on—and knowing it's only going to get worse from here, isn't exactly a consolation."

"It isn't a consolation for me, either," I said. "I don't look forward to knowing there's more blackouts and dissociation coming my way."

"Then why won't you just try medication?" Mike asked. "I

know you said you had doctors throw it at you before and expect a cure, and I get that it's not perfect. But maybe it's better than nothing?"

"Maybe," I muttered. "But you're ignoring the point entirely. It's not about whether I should be taking medication or not. It's about choice. And I'm making one."

"We've been over this," he shot back. "You make your choice, and I'll make mine. You stay off medication and continue hallucinating, I can't be with you."

"So how are we meant to move forward?" I asked.

"Kate, you mentioned before Mike arrived that there were some things you wanted to share with him," Naomi said. "Maybe that will help."

"I found a box full of journals, things I had filled out while dissociated," I said. "And it filled in some blanks. About fights we've had over the past year. We were never terribly happy, were we?"

"Everyone fights," he said. "That's just how couples are."

"In one of the journals, my alters said that you didn't keep your hands to yourself," I said. "I was worried about what that meant."

"This is ridiculous. You're telling me you're believing your hallucinations about something as serious as that?" Mike asked. "You can't trust anything written in those books. You really are far gone if you're actually listening to your imaginary friends."

"Do any of your other personalities have anything to say here, Kate?" Naomi asked.

I was fighting hard to not let Jer, Veronica, or Mila get too close to the front. I was trying to suppress and hide them, the way I had for the last year. But now that Naomi was asking directly, I felt I had to let them speak.

"Veronica never liked you, and you calling them my imaginary friends isn't helping," I admitted, surprised by how honest I was being. "Neither did Mila. She's scared of you. I think Jer supported our relationship only because he knew it made me happy, sometimes. But he seems to be on the fence about where he stands with you now."

"Jer? He?" Mike repeated. "You mean to tell me one of your personalities is a man?"

"Yeah," I said.

"This is crazy," he said, shaking his head. "You expect me to buy this crap?"

"Kate went through some trauma when she was young," Naomi said. "This means that her mind found comfort in creating alternative personalities for her, who would protect and defend her in the moments she needed them most. Combined with the wonderful imagination she has, she brought these people to life in her mind."

"Basically, you have this whole other life that I didn't know about," Mike said. "You're not the girl I thought I was dating."

"Mike!" I exclaimed. "I'm still the same person."

"But you're not. The person I fell in love with is just a piece of this puzzle. There's so much more to you than I even knew."

"Mike, I'm sensing you're feeling a lot of different emotions right now," Naomi said.

"I can't do this shit." Mike stood. "I'm sorry, but I can't. I won't sit here and be accused of things by people who don't even exist."

"Mike, wait—" I said.

He stormed out of Naomi's place.

"I'm so sorry about that," I said, after he was gone.

"It's all right," Naomi said. "We both knew he wasn't entirely prepared to be here."

"I think it's best that he left. He was getting really worked up."

"Do you need a moment to breathe?" Naomi asked.

"No, I should be okay. I want to use the remainder of our time to talk about those journals, though."

"What about them interests you?"

"They go back all the way to high school. Did you know about them?"

"Yes. Veronica loves journaling and would often bring it up. She mentioned how she kept all of her diaries, even from when she was a teenager."

"Is there some way we could use these journals to help me remember?" I asked. "Besides reading them, which I've been working on."

"It might be helpful for you to try and not only read the passages, but to put yourself back in time. To remember exactly how things went. How you felt. Where you felt it in your body. Feelings will help you unlock all the memories you've lost."

"I guess the question now is where to start," I said. "I have journals that go all the way back to 2009."

"Start whenever you feel is most important," Naomi said. "The rest will come on its own."

Chapter Six

November 2022

After my confession over text, I knew I had to set things right between Brielle and me. The bus ride to her apartment was nerve-racking. More than once, I thought I might hop off and make a run for it, but I stayed firmly planted in my seat. I fought my nerves. By the time I arrived at her building, my mouth was dry.

"Hey, it's me," I said, after dialing her number.

"Oh! Kate. Come up!" she said through the intercom.

I took the elevator up to her apartment. Once there, I knocked on the door.

Brielle opened the door. "Hey. Nice to see you. Come on in."

"Thanks." I stepped into the apartment.

I noticed that Brielle didn't hug me like usual but instead gave me a tight-lipped smile. That meant she probably wasn't totally unaffected by the text I had sent her. Maybe I had really messed things up.

I didn't even wait to sit down before I threw myself into it. "Look, I'm really sorry for the message I sent. It was totally wrong of me to send something like that over text. I was just really dissociated—"

"Shhh, it's okay," Brielle said. "I'm not mad at you. You can slow down. Breathe."

"You're not upset?" I asked. "Not at all?"

"I mean, I'm a little surprised. And I think it's worth talking about."

"Me, too." I motioned to myself. "Obviously. That's why I'm here."

"Do you think we can at least sit down for this talk?"

"Of course!"

We sat down on her couch. Her living room only had one piece of furniture in front of the TV. The blackout curtains were drawn, and a lamp was lit, giving the room a calming ambiance.

"I didn't expect everything to change so quickly," Brielle said. "How did we go from talking about your breakup with Mike, to how you have feelings for me now?"

"Things have been really weird for me, too," I said. "Sometimes I feel like I don't have control over the things I say. Even over text. I really am sorry for springing that on you."

"It's all right," Brielle said. "If you said it when you were dissociated, then does that mean you don't mean it?"

"I meant it, I just wish I had picked a better time or place for the talk."

"Well, here we are now." Brielle smiled, and this one went to her eyes. "And we can have the right kind of talk now."

"I promise you I had no idea how I felt until Veronica took

over." My words tumbled out fast. I had practiced a speech to Brielle in front of the mirror dozens of times, yet none of the words I'd rehearsed came out. "I sincerely looked at you only as a friend, until Mike broke up with me. Then it's like, I saw you in a new light…"

"And you think that you like me," Brielle concluded.

"I don't just *think* it. I know it."

Brielle placed a hand on mine. "I know the feelings might seem real, but you just went through a really hard time. Not only with your breakup, but the fight with Phoebe. You're probably feeling a lot of things right now and getting it all mixed up in your head."

"I wish that were the case. But I can tell you that my feelings for you are real."

Brielle's cheeks colored. "I don't know what to say. I mean, you know that I've had a crush on you since we were kids, right?"

"Really? I had no idea. You always had a new person on the go, I never suspected you liked me, too."

"I did. I totally did. Do you remember when we would sit together in biology class, and I'd let you read from my book? I was totally crushing on you. But after a few years of friendship, I accepted that you were probably straight."

"I don't know what I am," I said. "I'm hoping to figure that out along the way. All I know is I like you."

"And I feel the same way," Brielle said. "I guess the question now is: what do we do about it?"

"I'm probably too fresh out of my relationship to start dating again," I admitted. "And I should probably go to therapy again before I even try to start anything else."

"That sounds wise to me. And I mean, we need time to process. We might know each other really well, but not like that. In a romantic way."

"I dunno, I think you've been pretty romantic," I said. "Always looking out for me. Bringing me my favorite kinds of ice cream. Remembering what kinds of food make me sick. It's the little things."

"That's just how I show I care."

"That's good enough for me." I cleared my throat. "Anyway. I guess now that we've both expressed ourselves, we can table it for the time being. I'm in no way ready to date."

"But when you are..." Brielle smiled.

"I'll let you know," I said. "And we can see how things go from there."

"That sounds like a plan to me," Brielle replied. "And if you change your mind, that's no issue. I'll always be your friend."

I was reminded of Jer's words, of how he told me no matter what, Brielle would remain my friend. And he was right. Despite my awkward confession, we had managed to talk things out maturely and walk out of it with a solution.

"I'm really glad you're so understanding," I said. "Any other friend probably would have ended things right there."

"I've stood with you through worse than this," she said. "And hey, it worked out. Now you know how I feel. So, we're on the same page, right?"

"Right."

"I'm really proud of you for being upfront about your emotions lately. I've known you for so long now, and I have to say, it's not too often that I hear Kate Moore talk openly about her emotions. Especially difficult ones. You've tended to shy away from it."

"I'm trying to turn over a new leaf," I said. "Be more courageous."

"You're doing well so far," she said.

"Thank you."

"Have you told your mom about any of this?" Brielle asked. "I know she was fond of Mike."

"She was disappointed we'd broken up," I admitted. "Things have been so chaotic lately. I've barely had time to figure out who I am."

"Those sound like big questions. Do you think you'll tell your mom about what's going on with your mental health, too?"

I thought of how Phoebe had reacted. What if my mom reacted the same way? What if she thought it was all foolishness that I had dreamed up? I wasn't certain I could handle yet another rejection.

"I don't think so," I said. "She doesn't need to know about it."

"Whatever you choose to do, just know I'll support you," Brielle said.

"Thank you. And I'm sorry again for how I surprised you with that text message."

"Consider it ancient history. We've worked it out. There's nothing to be sorry for. And remember, I understand you were dissociated, and it didn't come out totally right. But it's okay to make mistakes. I won't end our friendship over that."

I hugged her. She hugged me back.

I stayed at Brielle's place for another two hours. She put on a pot of coffee and we listened to some records. Brielle loved to collect her favorite music on vinyl. She had bought her first record player when she was a teenager, and we had been listening to records together ever since.

When I got home, I noticed I had a missed call and a voicemail from Phoebe.

I decided to listen to it.

"Hey, Kate." Phoebe sighed. "Look, I wanted to say I'm really sorry for how things went down. I shouldn't have overreacted like that. I just didn't know how to process what you were telling me. I was scared for you, and I reacted in anger. Anyway, call me when you have a sec, okay?"

I called her back.

"Hey," she said when she picked up.

"Hi," I said. "I got your voicemail. Thank you for apologizing."

"You're welcome. It's the least I can do after how I behaved. I'm really sorry. You're going through something terrible, and I made a huge scene."

Wouldn't be the first time, part of me wanted to say, but I bit it back.

"It's okay, Phoebe. What matters is you're sorry, and you've said it. I really appreciate that."

"How do you manage to cope?" she asked. "With the breakup and then this?"

"I have good friends like Brielle by my side. She helps me through a lot of it."

"You two always were the closest out of our friend group. I'm glad you have each other."

"Me, too."

*

September 2010

I didn't expect to land in the principal's office. I had always been a model student. Straight A's. Always on time. I was hardly the kind of student you would expect to see waiting to talk to the principal. I had worked so hard to keep my image polished, for all of us. Kate had checked out a while ago, so it was up to me to take over.

"Ms. Moore?" the secretary called. "Mr. Rindhald will see you now."

I went into his office with my shoulders slumped. I had already admitted defeat.

"Please, Kate, sit down," Mr. Rindhald said.

I took a seat in front of his desk. "Thanks."

"Now, can you tell me more about what happened between you and Analise?" Mr. Rindhald asked.

I crossed my arms in front of my chest. "She was being rude. I simply put her in her place."

"And how was she being rude, Ms. Moore?"

"She was saying slurs, sir," I replied, anger still hot on my tongue. "She called one of the boys in the class...well, a word that means gay."

"So, you were standing up for your classmate when you shoved her over her desk and nearly broke her nose?"

"I was defending him, yes," I muttered. "I didn't mean to shove her *that* hard."

"Kate, I'll be honest with you. This is the first time we've seen you behave this way. I have to wonder if there's more going on here. How are things at home?"

I balled my hands into fists. "That's none of your business."

"The school prides itself on taking care of its students—"

"You won't be able to take care of me," I shot back. "Sorry, but there's no great explanation for why I acted the way I did. I'm no different than usual. She just really got on my nerves. I find slurs like that to be unacceptable."

"And you're right, Kate, they are unacceptable," the principal said. "But the school also has a zero-tolerance policy for violence. You understand what this means, right?"

"That I'm suspended," I said lamely.

"I don't know that we'll go as far as a suspension, but you'll have to miss your lunches and spend your free periods under supervision. Does that seem fair?"

"It is what it is," I mumbled.

"All right. I hope you know Analise's parents expect an apology for the injuries you caused their daughter."

"Did they also raise her to be a homophobic prick?" I asked.

"Please, language. Kate, I have known you for years now. This is really unlike you. Why don't you go take a walk and cool down?"

"Sounds great," I snapped.

I left the office as soon as I was able. I stomped down the hallway to my locker. Brielle was there waiting for me.

"How did it go?" she asked. "Did he suspend you for breaking Analise's nose?"

"It's not broken," I muttered, inputting my lock passcode. "She's pissed, though. Her parents want a formal apology from me."

"That's bullshit," Brielle said. "If they could have heard their daughter in class, they wouldn't be so keen to defend her. The way she talked to Paul was horrid."

"They probably taught her to talk that way." I opened my locker and grabbed my backpack. "What really grinds my gears is that they think I'm the problem. Me! The golden student. How many awards have I won for this place? One bad day, and then they throw it all away?"

"I don't think they'll throw it all away over this. Did they suspend you?"

"No, just said I'd need supervision during my free periods."

"At least you can still come to school."

"Yay," I said flatly. "Now I can be like an actual prisoner with guards and everything. Do you think people will whisper about me? Kate, the bully. Kate, the girl-shover."

"I don't think anyone will say much, beyond how much it sucked that Analise had to talk like that," Brielle said. "And I know Paul really appreciated you stepping up for him."

"You know, I barely even remember it happening. I remember her saying all that mean stuff, and then…nothing. The next thing I remember, I'm sitting in the principal's office."

"But you remember the slurs?"

"Yeah, and I remember thinking *someone should do something about this*."

"And then you did."

"Yeah, guess I did." I shoved my books in my backpack. "But I don't remember doing it. Guess I need some sleep."

"It's the first time I've seen you angry enough to lash out at someone like that," Brielle said. "Well, someone that wasn't your dad, I mean."

"I don't know what's up with me, Bri," I said. "Maybe I'm PMS-ing."

"Maybe." Her eyes still looked worried. "Do you think you'll be able to make it out to rehearsal tonight?"

"I'm banned from practice. Besides, Dad is going to be here soon to pick me up."

Brielle smiled. "Okay. Stay strong. I'm just a phone call away if you need me."

"See you."

When Brielle left, I slammed my locker closed. I intended to spend the evening working out, to get rid of all of this pent-up energy I felt inside. Reading lines and pretending everything was okay wasn't going to be enjoyable for me, so I was glad that I had to miss rehearsal.

I looked up from my locker. Analise stood a few feet away from me, her face red.

"There you are," she said.

"I haven't been hiding," I replied.

"Well, I've been looking for you. I have some things to say to you."

"Nothing I want to hear." I turned away.

"Come back here!" she yelled.

I ignored her and kept moving down the hallway. I heard the slap of her flats on the floor as she chased after me.

"Kate!" she said.

I stopped. "What? You want an apology? I'm not going to give you one."

"It was my parents who asked for that. Although saying you're sorry for knocking me over wouldn't hurt."

"I didn't mean to mess up your face," I said, though I didn't sound very apologetic. I added, "I'm sorry."

"I came back to school because I wanted to say this to your face," Analise said. "I'm sorry, too. For saying all that stuff about Paul in class."

"Maybe it's not me you should be apologizing to. Though I'm surprised to hear you say sorry at all after my meeting with the principal."

"Like I said, my parents were the ones who were the angriest. I just wanted you to know that I won't be speaking like that to him again."

"I don't believe you," I said flatly.

"It's the last time you'll hear me say those words," Analise said. "I promise."

"Why do you think it's funny to make fun of someone for being gay?" Anger pulsed through my veins to my hands, which were balled up in fists at my side. I wanted to yell, but I kept my tone even.

"Paul can be kind of obnoxious about it. I don't mean to be a homophobe, but he's always talking about gay rights. Can't he talk about something else for once?"

My eyes must have indicated that I was not the right person to complain to. "You don't know what you're talking about."

"Don't you ever find it kind of annoying, though?" Analise asked. "You can see where I'm coming from."

"No, I can't," I shot back. "I don't think talking about his human rights is annoying at all. It makes sense that gay rights would be on his mind when he's, you know, gay."

"I mean, I guess," Analise muttered.

I fought the urge to shove her onto her face a second time.

"What if I told you that I was gay?" I asked. "What if I told you that when you speak badly against him, you speak badly against me, too?"

"You are?" Analise stuttered. She recovered quickly. "Well, even if you are, you're not one of those annoying gays. You're the right kind. The kind that keeps quiet about all that pride stuff."

"That's such bullshit," I said. "Do you hear how homophobic you sound right now?"

"I'm not homophobic!" Analise exclaimed. She looked me up and down with disgust. "I'm just being realistic. Maybe you aren't a reasonable type of lezzie after all."

"Don't call me that," I growled.

Analise looked scared for a moment. She took a few steps back. "If you push me again, I'll make sure this is the last time you step foot in this school. My parents are already asking for you to be removed from class entirely."

"And if you don't stop spouting that homophobic crap, I'm

going to make sure you don't step back into class recognizable as yourself anymore," I snapped.

Analise gasped. "You wouldn't."

"Don't try me. I think we're done talking here, don't you?"

"You're crazy," she said. "You have crazy eyes. I'm out of here."

I breathed a sigh of relief when she was gone. I turned on my heels and headed out the doors on the opposite end of the hall.

Dad was outside waiting for me in the car. By the look on his face, I knew I was going to be chewed out before I even got in. The sun was still high in the sky, and the birds were singing. But despite the lovely day, I knew things were going to get ugly. The walk between the school and the car was the calm before the storm.

"What the hell was this stunt, Kate?" Dad asked as soon as I got into the car.

"It wasn't a stunt," I muttered.

Dad started the car. "Your principal called to say you got into a fight at school."

"Yeah, well. She deserved it."

"What the hell!" He locked the doors and started driving. "So, this is the kind of young woman I've raised? The kind who thinks it's okay to fight at school?"

I fought the urge to tell him he didn't raise me at all. That had been Mom. He had barely been present enough to mark the passing years.

"Just because you're picking me up today doesn't mean you have to actually act like a father and scold me," I said.

"Do not be short with me right now, miss," Dad snapped.

"I've accepted my punishment from the school. I've talked to Analise and said sorry. Can't we just leave it there?"

"Leave it there? You think we can just leave it there? How do you expect you'll ever keep a job as an adult if you're stuck in jail?"

"I'm not going to prison, Dad."

"No, but if you continue with this kind of behavior, they could throw you in there with charges. And then your life is ruined. This is what you want?"

"No," I ground out through clenched teeth.

"Then you better fuckin' smarten up," he said. "Or else you're going to be on your own."

I was tempted to ask him what he meant by that, but I bit it back down. I could picture Jer in the back seat. My imaginary friend. Always there to comfort me. I definitely needed him now.

"It's best if you don't push him right now," Jer said. "He'll only get angrier, and when you get home you might regret it."

Even if Dad was in a worse mood when I got home, what was he going to do? He didn't hit me anymore. That had ended a few years ago. All he could do was yell and insult me, and he had been doing that my entire life. I took a few deep breaths and focused on the houses passing by.

"Your mother is so disappointed in you," Dad said. He didn't speak again the rest of the way.

When we got home, Mom was waiting for us in the kitchen. She had her arms crossed in front of her chest. The phone was sitting on the table, as if she had just put it down.

"Was it worth it, Kate?" Mom asked.

I took off my coat and shoes. "No. It wasn't."

"Then you regret what you did?"

"Do you even *know* why I shoved her?"

"I heard she was pestering one of your classmates," Mom said.

"It was more than that. She was calling him homophobic slurs."

"Oh goodness. That wasn't very nice. But you still shouldn't have fought her."

"I didn't intend to!" I insisted. "I thought I'd push her a little to get her to knock it off."

"You did far more than that," Mom said. "She nearly broke her nose."

"I don't remember shoving her that hard." I shook my head. "I don't really remember it at all. I was so angry."

"Paul isn't even your friend, honey. Why would you put yourself in the line of fire for him?"

"Because she was being homophobic, Mom!" I exclaimed. "I can't just let people get away with that."

"We have plenty of family members who don't approve of the gay lifestyle, but you've never gone and shoved them, now have you?"

I was shaking with anger. "No. I haven't."

"Then you must know that using some tact and diplomacy is always better than violence," Mom said.

"I do know that, yes," I said.

"Then why did you act the way you did?" Dad asked.

I considered coming out to them. It would probably shock them out of their anger and into a different kind of emotion. Likely disbelief, confusion, and maybe frustration. But Kate wasn't gay. I had told Analise she was as a way to get her to back off, but I wasn't sure I wanted to mess with Kate's life this way. Coming out as a lesbian to Mom and Dad would only confuse things when Kate snapped out of her dissociation and took control again.

"I guess I care about social justice," I muttered. "More than I used to."

"Well, as you probably expect, you're grounded," Mom said. "You can go to your room. No rehearsals this week, and no time with Brielle."

"Fine," I said.

I went up to my room before my parents could see me crying. It was hard to be their daughter. They didn't realize that the person they were speaking to wasn't always Kate. Didn't always have the same thoughts and feelings as Kate. Shouldn't be expected to do all the things that Kate did. I hadn't even bothered to try to act like her today, not when everyone was already so explosively angry at me for defending not only Paul, but myself.

I turned on my computer and logged into Facebook Messenger. I knew it was only a matter of time before my parents banned me from using my computer, but for now I still had my laptop. I sent a message to Brielle to let her know how things were going. I would call her later to give her the full update on how my parents had reacted. There was also a message from Paul.

> ***Paul:*** *Thanks for today, Kate. I know that can't have been easy. I'm really sorry you got in trouble because of me.*
>
> ***Me:*** *You're welcome. I'd do it again. Don't worry about it. You deserve better than that.*
>
> ***Paul:*** *You're my hero.*

I stared at my screen in shock. His hero. I had never imagined that acting out the way I had would land me the title. But he seemed really grateful that I had gotten her off his case, hopefully permanently.

> ***Me:*** *I just hope she leaves you alone now. Stay safe, okay?*

I stood up and moved over to the mirror hanging from my wall. My face seemed wrong. My hair was flat against my face and a bit frizzy from the humidity. My lips seemed to slant down in a way they didn't usually. My eyes were red and puffy from crying. But there was rage within them, rage that didn't belong to Kate.

When she finally came to, she was going to be devastated at being semi-suspended. I took out my journal from where I kept it hidden in a box under the bed. I opened it and started writing.

*

I was grounded by my mom for two weeks, and when I was at school, all my free time was supervised. By the end of it, I was relieved to see Brielle. She seemed relieved to see me, too, because she gave me a massive hug when I got to school. We were standing in front of the doors. Brielle was wearing ripped jeans and a band T-shirt. I wore black pants and a burgundy top, with my hair pulled back.

"I know I've said this before over the phone, but I'm so proud of you for sticking up for Paul the way you did," Brielle said. "Analise has left him alone entirely."

"I'm glad to hear it," I said.

"You know, there's something I wanted to tell you about all this. Because it wasn't just Paul you were defending, when you hit her. It was me, too."

"What do you mean?" I asked.

"I'm gay, too," Brielle said plainly.

"Brielle, really?" I asked, unable to keep the shock out of my voice. "I had no idea."

"I knew I could trust you with this, especially after you stood up for Paul the way you did."

"Of course you can trust me."

"People have started to say we're a couple. Because apparently Analise thinks you're gay, too."

"Let them say what they want," I said. "It doesn't change a thing."

"So, you don't mind if they think we're together?" Brielle asked, her face coloring slightly.

"No, why would I? What matters is you and I know the truth. And I'm so glad you could trust me with it."

I hugged her tightly. She smiled. "Yeah. We know the truth."

*

November 2022

"How's your drink?" Brielle asked.

She sat across from me in a booth at a quaint little pub. A night out felt warranted after all the stress I had been through recently. Normally I didn't like going out for drinks, but the place she had picked was clean, and the staff was friendly. Next to me in the booth was my violin case and some sheet music. We had chosen this pub not only because it was quaint, but because they hosted an open mic night every second week.

"The cider here is good," I told her, with a half-hearted smile.

"But *you're* not feeling good, are you?"

"It has nothing to do with where we are. You picked a great little spot. I like how calm it is."

"At least we're here together, right? As opposed to you being at home alone feeling this way."

"Yeah," I said, with a genuine smile this time. "At least we're here together."

"Do you think you'll play tonight?" she asked, motioning to my violin case.

"Depends on how nervous I am. Playing the piano for you was one thing, but I haven't performed in forever."

"But you have me here to support you. And Jer and Veronica are probably kicking around here, too, aren't they?"

"They're here." I looked at Veronica and Jer, who stood near our booth.

"And we hope you go up on stage, too," Jer said.

"They're supportive, too," I told Brielle. "Well, at least Jer is. Veronica's too busy glaring at all the other patrons."

"I'm not *glaring*," Veronica said. "I'm scanning the crowd to make sure there's nobody here we want to avoid."

"I think performing here would be a good challenge for me," I said. "The crowd isn't too big. My nerves won't be shattered. I'm just a little anxious."

"You'll do great, I just know it," Brielle said.

I signed up to perform, then returned to my seat in the booth. Brielle and I listened to a few singer-songwriters perform on stage. Most were accompanied by their guitars. Another musician played a lap harp. They were all very good, and by the time it was my turn to go up, my limbs felt like jelly. I was a classically trained musician, but I had never been able to shake my stage fright. I reminded myself that my best friend was there to watch over me, and so were my alters. *I'm not alone.*

I got up on stage. A few people clapped politely. I set my violin case down, opened it, and pulled out my instrument. I adjusted it on my shoulder and tested the strings. I approached the mic.

"Hello, everyone," I said. "I'd like to dedicate this song to my best friend."

I heard Brielle give a faint whoop before the room fell silent in anticipation.

"This is an original song, titled *Storm*," I said. "I hope you like it."

I pulled on Veronica's presence in my mind. She was no longer standing by Brielle. She was inside my mind now, controlling my movements, organizing my thoughts. Jer stood at a distance, watching intently, a smile of encouragement on his face. Alone, I was hopeless. But together, we could do this.

I played. My bowing was frenzied, my fingers skipping over the strings with fervor. I had hoped to encapsulate my feelings of disorientation and fear in this piece. My body moved with the music, my brow furrowed. An inspiration of mine for this song had been Vivaldi, although to my ears it sounded much more erratic and less refined than the master composer. Nearing the end, I slowed the tempo, hitting a few final, mournful notes.

The room was filled with cheers and people clapping. I put my instrument back in its case and returned nervously to my seat. All the confidence that had been present when I was playing vanished, and I was back to just being Kate again.

"You did so well!" Brielle exclaimed as I sat. "I'm so proud of you! That song is amazing. I can't believe you wrote it yourself."

"Thank you," I said.

A waitress approached us with a glass of wine. "This was sent to you by the lady at the front."

"Oh!" I exclaimed, surprised. "Thank you."

When the waitress walked away, both Brielle and I turned around in the booth to get a better look at the woman who had sent me the glass of wine. She sat at a table next to the stage. Her hair was so blonde it was almost white. She wore dark-red lipstick that really popped against the contrast of her pale skin and hair. She was dressed in a white button-up top, tight-fitting white skirt, and black pumps. She was clearly a woman with money. I wondered how much the glass of wine had cost.

The woman caught us looking at her and waved. I waved back, as a sign of thanks, and turned to Brielle.

"She must've really enjoyed the performance," I said.

"Well, you'll be able to find out soon," Brielle responded. "She's heading over here now."

When she reached our booth, the mysterious woman reached out her hand in greeting.

"Hello," she said. "My name is Hilda."

"Nice to meet you." I shook her hand. "My name is Kate, and this is Brielle."

"A pleasure to meet you both," Hilda said. "You play extremely well, Kate. You must be a professional musician."

"I am," I said.

"What brings you to a place like this? Shouldn't you be performing for a larger crowd?" Hilda asked.

"The truth is, I've struggled with stage fright my entire life," I told her. "I barely passed my examinations as a kid because I couldn't stand playing in front of more than a few people."

"Ah, so you are being courageous by coming out here and facing your fear," Hilda said. "How very admirable."

"Thank you." Blush crept up my neck. "I wish I could do more, but for now, the pub is where I start challenging myself."

"Your song was wonderful," Hilda said. "I've actually been searching for a violinist to play for my boss. He's a busy man and doesn't have time to come out to music nights, but I like to think of this as a bit of scouting. What are your rates like for a private concert?"

I had to fight not to gape. I had never been approached like this before. I didn't want to tell her I hadn't worked out my rates for private concerts, since I usually had requests for songs to be created digitally rather than for live performances. "I suppose that's something that could be worked out between him and me."

"Cost is not an issue, if that's why you're hesitating," Hilda said. "Isaac is quite well off. He can afford your rates."

"That sounds great to me," I said. "What kind of music would he like to hear?"

"He likes all sorts. Although whatever you have written yourself would be a delight. He's always looking for new music, and from what I heard tonight, you've got exactly the style I've been searching for."

"I'm really glad to hear that."

"Here's my card." Hilda handed me her business card. "Send me a text tonight, and I'll give you the details. Would tomorrow be too early for a private concert?"

Tomorrow. That barely gave me time to prepare. Veronica answered for me. "Of course not. We'll be ready by then."

"Excellent," Hilda said, either not hearing or ignoring the use of "we". "If you perform even half as well as you did tonight, he'll be impressed. You can expect a nice tip. And maybe a bottle of wine."

"Thank you so much," I said. "I'll be in touch."

"Have a good night, ladies," Hilda said, then walked out of the pub.

"Can you believe that?" Brielle asked. She was practically jumping in her seat. "You got a gig! I knew coming out tonight was a good idea. If you had stayed home, who knows if you would have gotten a request to perform from some wealthy patron!"

"I know next to nothing about this guy," I said, and I knew it was Veronica still speaking through me. "I hope he's a good boss."

"You can handle yourself. You've done private concerts before. And if you need someone to be there with you, I can take some time off work and go with you."

"That would be great, actually. It would help to have you there. You were a big support tonight and I couldn't have done it without you."

"Thank you. I thought it was really sweet how you dedicated the song to me," Brielle said. "Nobody's ever done that before."

"You're welcome," I said, and squeezed her hand.

We spent the rest of the night listening to the musicians who followed. I couldn't help but peek at the business card Hilda had given me. Her official title was administrative assistant, but I could tell she did much more than that if she was scouting for her boss, too. I knew next to nothing about him—only his name. Isaac Reynolds.

I hoped he was a pleasant person to work for.

"Only one way to find out," Jer said. "And look on the bright side, Brielle said she would go with you."

I tried to focus on that fact. I wasn't alone.

*

The next day, we stood in front of what looked to me like a castle. It was a five-story mansion with a gated entryway. Brielle had driven us both over, and we had parked the car and walked trepidatiously to the front door. Hilda greeted us when we knocked.

"So glad you could make it," she said, when she opened the door. "And welcome to you as well, Brielle."

"Glad to be here," I said, trying not to clutch my violin case too hard.

"Isaac is just upstairs," Hilda said. "Let me lead the way."

We followed her into the house. She was dressed all in white again. This time she was wearing long, flowing white pants and a tight-fitting white top. Those familiar black pumps were still there, and her heels clacked against the tiled floor.

We made our way up the stairs and through winding hallways to Isaac's office. The walls seemed almost cavernous on the inside, bending inward. They were painted white. I sensed a theme. The path, despite its oddly shaped walls, was straight and narrow. The design of the mansion seemed to me like something out of a story book. It gave the illusion of walking through a cavern.

When we made it to Isaac's door, Hilda held up a hand. "One moment, please."

She entered the room, leaving Brielle and me alone in the hallway for a moment.

"Quite the place, isn't it?" Brielle said. Her voice seemed to echo in the confined space. She lowered her tone. "This guy must be loaded to have it all designed like this."

"I'd like to know his inspiration," I whispered back. "It's giving me cave vibes. But why all the white?"

Hilda reappeared before Brielle could answer. "I'm sorry, ladies, but it seems like there's been a bit of a miscommunication. Isaac only wants to see Kate. I'm afraid that means you'll have to head home, Brielle."

Brielle's face fell, and her eyes met mine in a moment of panic. "But I told Kate I'd be there for her."

"We can arrange to have you sent home," Hilda said. "If you need a lift."

"No, that's okay, I drove here," Brielle said, then turned back to me. "Are you okay with this?"

"I…" I paused. I had hoped to have my best friend by my side while I performed. That had been the only thing holding me together up until this point. "I don't know why you can't come in with me."

"Isaac is very particular about who he lets visit," Hilda said, and a line of worry creased her perfect forehead. "Given that he only invited you, Kate, he's uncertain Brielle's vibes would match your own. And that's something he cares a great deal about."

Hearing someone as elegant and sophisticated as Hilda talk about "vibes" seemed almost comical, but I didn't laugh. Brielle looked like she was ready to put up a fight, but I didn't want to make things more difficult than they already were.

"It's all right, I'll go in alone," I said. I looked at Brielle. "I'll call you as soon as I'm out and give you an update, okay?"

Brielle worried her lip with her teeth. "Okay. Please do."

"This way, if you please," Hilda said, and put a guiding hand on Brielle's back.

I opened the door to Isaac's office and walked in.

Isaac's office space was immaculately clean. There was a desk, pristinely polished, in the corner of the room, with a desktop computer. Two large French windows were draped with white curtains that blew slightly in the breeze. The man in question was lying on a four-seater white leather couch. His clothes were the opposite of everything in the room—they were stained with white paint. He wore a plain brown shirt with tattered denim jeans. He had his head resting on the arm of the couch. His hair was mostly black, with a few gray streaks, and he didn't have any lines on his face. His expression was stern. He appeared to be in his mid-fifties.

"So, *you're* the famous violinist I've heard so much about," Isaac said, without looking at me. He stared at the phone in his hands.

"I'm not famous," I replied. "I'm just Kate."

He looked at me for the first time. "You know, I find that hard to believe."

"Pardon?"

"That you're 'just Kate.' Hilda doesn't pick just anyone to play for me." He looked me up and down. His gaze hovered over my violin case. "So, show me what you've got."

"I have a few songs prepared—"

"No, no, no. I don't want your pre-programmed stuff. I want all the originals. It'd be even better if you could improvise it on the spot."

I hesitated. "Improvise? I don't know…"

"Please don't say no." Isaac looked up from his phone again. "I know you can do it—Hilda told me as much. Do you not want to play for me?"

I was at a loss for words, so I said nothing.

"You know, you're quite beautiful."

"Thank you." The compliment, coming out of the blue from a man I barely knew, should have made me uncomfortable, but Isaac seemed more charming than creepy. His smile was disarming. I motioned to my violin case. "Should I try to play you some songs now? I can't promise they'll be any good, but I'll do my best."

"Hilda recorded everyone's performances last night and sent them to me." He turned his phone screen toward me, showing me a video playing on mute. The video was of me playing at the pub. "This song was so good. Could you play more like that?"

"I can definitely try." My muscles tensed up. Despite him being only one person, my stage fright was acting up again.

"No—you know what? I don't think I'm in the mood for music."

"Oh…then…should I go?" I asked.

Veronica stood by the door, her arms crossed in front of her chest. "I don't trust this guy."

"Give him a chance," I wanted to say, but kept that thought to myself.

"Stay," Isaac said. "I think your performance last night was enough to prove you're good at this. How about I book you for my next event? I have a few coming up in the next couple months. It would mean a fair amount of work for you, and a fair amount of pay."

"If you don't mind me asking..." Veronica pulled at my consciousness. I let her take over. I was too nervous to speak my mind. I cleared my throat. "But if you already knew you were going to hire me based on the video, why ask me to come here today at all?"

"Because I needed to meet you to get your vibe. Now that I've gotten a better sense of you, I know you'd make a good fit as part of my team."

"You have a very impressive place here. What kind of business are you in?" Veronica asked.

"I'm a philosopher," he said. "I write books. People buy them. I'll have some copies sent home with you today so you can read them. It will benefit you to know more about my whole way of life." He smiled. "You know, you'd be an excellent face for my brand."

"Like a model?" I asked. "Sorry, but I don't pose for photos. I'm not very photogenic, anyway."

"Well, you might change your mind once you've read *Rest and Longing*. That's my latest book."

"We'll see," I said. "I really feel I should at least play one piece for you. I was invited here to play you something."

"Think of this less as a concert and more like an interview. And you passed with flying colors." He sat up and waved his hands as if to dismiss me. "Don't worry about trying to impress me with your musical talent. You've already done that with your performance from last night."

"Why not tell me this was a test?" I heard Veronica ask through me. "If I had known, I could have prepared better," she added, trying to save face.

"You did fine, darling. You did excellent, in fact. You're going to make loads of money at my events. People will love you."

"At least I'll have my set prepared," I said, motioning to my instrument.

"Oh no, I'll tell you what to play. You'll barely need to lift a finger." He laughed at his own joke. "Get it? Because you're a violinist."

I smiled.

"You're much prettier when you smile," he observed. "D'you know that?"

I blushed. "Thank you."

Isaac laughed. "I like you. I think you're going to do great here."

I noticed that he hadn't even asked me if I wanted the job. He had assumed I would. And, being desperate for work, I didn't have much of a choice but to accept by omission.

"You've got a week," Isaac said. "A week to prepare some original music for my next reading. It'll be here. I can send a car for you, so you don't need to worry about traveling. I'll send you something nice to wear. Something white."

"I noticed Hilda only ever seems to wear white," I said. "Is there a reason for that?"

"It has to do with how we present ourselves to the world. White is the color of purity and light. We pursue light in all that we do. Even your music, Kate, is in pursuit of the Light. You'll understand more once you've read my book. Trust me."

"We could at least read his book," Jer said. "Who knows what might be in there."

"All that talk about purity and light—*ugh*." Veronica shook her head. "There's no way there's anything valuable in there."

"Thank you for your time," I said to Isaac. "I'll be in touch."

"Yes, you will," Isaac replied with a broad smile.

I hurried out of his office. Hilda waited for me in the hallway, as if she had been standing guard by the door.

"How did it go?" she asked, with a nervous smile.

"It went well," I said.

Hilda tapped on her phone a few times, then smiled. "I just got his text message about it. He'll be sorting out an outfit for you, so you don't have to do anything. I have this covered, don't even worry about it."

Had he texted her *that* quickly? I looked back to the closed door. He must have lightning-fast texting skills.

"Seems he runs a pretty tight ship around here," I commented.

"We like to keep on top of things," Hilda replied, her nerves vanishing. "I'm so glad to hear the meeting went well. I knew when I saw you perform on stage you'd be the perfect musician for his events."

"He mentioned it was a reading of his books. Does he do many of those?" I asked.

"Once a week. Usually on Tuesdays."

I wondered if there was a reason for this, but assumed I would find out more once I read *Rest and Longing*, as I had been told multiple times. Hilda handed me a copy with a smile. I smiled back, hesitantly, feeling I was stepping into unknown waters. I was uncertain about my ability to navigate my way through.

Chapter Seven

November 2022

I closed Isaac's book.

"This book is...pretty hard to read," I said and set it aside on the bed.

"What did you expect?" Veronica asked from where she sat next to me. "Some literary masterpiece? The guy didn't exactly seem like America's Next Top Philosopher, if you know what I mean."

"Work is work, and we've only just met him." I paused. "I think he was nice."

"Nice? Really? Try 'creepy.' And what's with this whole 'white is the color of purity' crap? Doesn't that seem a bit racist to begin with?" Veronica sneered.

"It's not great...basing an idea of purity off a color," I admitted. "It's definitely gone wrong in history before. You have a point.

Jer, what's your take on all of this?"

"I'm with you both here," Jer replied. "I think we should keep our guard up, but if the gig goes well, it's a pretty great opportunity."

"He told me I'd understand more about him once I read his book." I threw up my hands. "I feel more lost now than before I read it. I don't really know what it means to be an Independent."

"Philosophy is a dense subject," Jer said.

"*His* version of philosophy is denser, even," Veronica said. "Because it's mostly just gibberish meant to appeal to people who think you can cure depression with positive thought. It's offensive, frankly. And I like to think we're a bit more scientifically minded than that."

"The parts on positive thought did seem a bit out there," I said. "But it's nothing I haven't read in any other religious text about prayer."

"So, you're going through with it, then," Veronica said.

"It's work," I replied. "I don't have to agree with it, I just have to do the job."

"Well, haven't you become Miss Practical," Veronica remarked.

"I don't really have anything to wear," I said.

"You could wear the dress Hilda sent," Veronica suggested.

"The neckline plunges a bit too much for my comfort," I said. "But I might not have a choice. It's not like I own any outfits all in white. And both she and Isaac were pretty clear about the dress code being mandatory."

"What are they going to do if you show up dressed in black?" Veronica asked. "Strip you naked in front of everyone?"

"No way! They would never do that. They're too nice," I said.

"They might ask you to change, at the very least, in that

situation," Jer said. "I imagine they keep spares on hand for cases like that."

"No way they have dozens of dresses like this one lying around, though," I said, looking to where the white gown hung from my door. "It looks pretty expensive. It feels like it, too."

"How can something *feel* expensive?" Veronica asked.

"It's made from something other than polyester. And it's not so thin it's basically see-through. That's how." I got up from bed and walked over to the dress. "I'll do it. I'll wear the dress Hilda picked out for me to the event."

"Let's not delude ourselves, though," Veronica said. "Do you really think Hilda picked it out? Or is Isaac the more likely culprit?"

"With the plunging neckline, I suspect you have a point," Jer said. "What if he's trying to flirt with you?"

"It's possible," I said, remembering all the compliments he'd paid me on our first meeting. "I just have to get in, keep my head down, and get the job done. Play the songs he wanted. Originals. And then leave."

I got changed into the white gown. I ignored my instinct to cover up with a cardigan—I didn't have any white ones. I glanced at myself in the mirror. I combed my fingers through my hair, brushing it forward over my shoulders. After applying a bit of makeup, I felt ready for the event.

*

Hilda greeted me outside the mansion as soon as I stepped out of the car they had sent for me.

"Kate! Hi!" Hilda said. "Glad you could make it. And good timing, too. Isaac is still getting ready upstairs. We can sneak you in."

"I like to arrive at work early," I said. "Thankfully the driver you sent had the same thought."

"Perfect. I like that about you!" Hilda said. She put a hand to the small of my back and guided me toward the front entrance. "Isaac will want to speak with you when he can. He'll definitely be in touch with you before the night is done."

"Great," I said.

We walked through the massive doorway. Hilda led me to the living space, where a stage had been prepared. There was a podium with a microphone.

"Should I set up here?" I asked.

"I've cleared a space for you to the right of the stage," Hilda said with an encouraging smile. "You'll do great tonight! Just remember to breathe. If you do half as well as you did at the pub, you'll have a few fans by the end of the night. Mark my words!"

With that, she left me to get ready on my own. I set down my violin case and arranged my sheet music. I didn't strictly need to do this, as I was already prepared, but I wanted to look busy as the guests arrived. As they walked in, they seemed wholly uninterested in me, their eyes darting around the room, likely looking for the star of the show, who hadn't yet made his appearance. I noticed that most guests were clutching copies of Isaac's new book. They really *were* fans.

I spotted Isaac as soon as he entered the room. He seemed far cleaner and more put together than when I first met him. He wore a well-fitting white suit. He looked handsome.

Hilda gave me a thumbs-up, and I took that as my cue to start my performance. I played two original songs as Isaac mingled with guests. When he got on stage, I stopped.

"Thank you, everyone, for coming out tonight," he said into the mic. The lights dimmed and a spotlight shone on him. "Let us begin with the Affirmations. 'I am strong. I am capable. I need only myself—and myself is the Light.'"

The crowd repeated his words. Isaac closed his eyes, his lips moving, but not speaking. The crowd mimicked him, lost in the moment. *These people really look to him as a spiritual leader.*

Once the prayer was over, Isaac read a passage from his book. It was the section on the importance of sobriety and dedicating yourself to the Light. He emphasized the need to stay on the Path, and to not stray from it. His audience was listening intently, hanging on his every word.

I resumed playing once the reading was over. Another original, this one inspired by Lindsay Sterling. It was lively, and it got me a few looks. The crowd moved away from me as Isaac approached.

"How is my star violinist doing tonight?" he asked.

"Well, thank you," I said, uncertain how to take the compliment. "And you?"

"I'm radiant. Can't you tell?" He laughed. "Loosen up, Kate. I'm teasing you."

"Of course," I muttered. "Guess I'm a bit tense from the stage fright. I still have that, although it's getting easier the more I play."

"You have nothing to worry about. Some very, *very* important people are here tonight. And they were all impressed by you and your obvious talent."

"I'm flattered," I said.

"But I think most of the attention you got was because of your dress. I think I did a good job picking it out, didn't I?"

"It's beautiful."

"It belonged to my wife," Isaac said. "It was a shame to see it sitting in a closet, unworn. It deserves to be worn, don't you think?"

"Oh, wow." I paused. "I had no idea. I thought it was new."

"We've taken great care of her things since she passed," he said.

For the first time that night, Veronica appeared. She stood next to Isaac.

"His wife passed?" Veronica said, shocked.

"Where do you go? When you look away like that..." Isaac said.

"Oh, do I? I'm sorry." I knew I sounded anxious. "I don't mean to zone out on you."

"When you're nervous, you space out. Go somewhere else in your mind. I've noticed."

"I guess sometimes it happens when I'm nervous."

"This guy is really intense," Veronica said. "I could *not* work with him."

I ignored Veronica. He was too observant. He would notice if I "went away" again.

"You're shaking," he remarked, placing a hand on my arm. His voice was soothing. "You poor thing."

"I guess I'm a little cold," I said.

"Probably from the door being left wide open," Isaac said. "Hilda! Let's get everyone out and close the doors."

The guests had all but left. A few people hovered nearby, waiting to speak with Isaac. I recognized one of the faces.

It was Mike.

"Do you know him?" I asked. "The tall, blond guy." He was the last person I'd expected to see tonight.

"Who, Mike?" Isaac asked, a little surprised. "Yeah, great guy. He's new. How do *you* know him?"

"We used to be close," I said, uncertain on how to phrase it.

"Used to be... I take it things didn't work out between you

two," Isaac said.

"Pretty much," I replied.

Before I could make my escape, Mike spotted me and made a beeline over toward Isaac and me. I looked nervously at Isaac, but he smiled at me.

"Get out of there!" Veronica yelled. Her scream filled my entire mind, but there was nowhere for me to go.

"I can't," I whispered weakly.

Moments later, Mike was standing in front of me. He had a fresh haircut, and he wore white pants with a casual white T-shirt. Far less dressed up than Isaac standing at my side. Mike's expression looked torn between awe for Isaac and frustration at seeing me.

"Hey," he said, looking at me.

"Hi," I replied.

Isaac linked his arm in mine. "Mike, great to see you. I take it you two know each other?"

I didn't pull my arm away. I knew Isaac was offering me some kind of protection here, from Mike.

"Yeah, we know each other," Mike said. "Although I'd steer clear from her if I were you."

"I don't see why," Isaac replied. "Kate's been a perfect entertainer tonight. She played wonderfully. And she's great company, too. Although I suspect you already knew something about that."

Mike blinked. "I guess I do."

"Why didn't you ever tell me you were involved with this group?" Veronica asked through me in an accusatory tone. I could feel my identity shifting. I didn't have a firm grip on who I was right now, and it was giving Veronica freedom to take control.

"Because I didn't think it was something you'd be interested in," he said. He looked pointedly at my arm, linked with Isaac's.

"Clearly I was wrong."

"Kate was here purely as a working musician," Isaac said. "She hasn't joined us yet."

The way he emphasized "yet" gave me pause. He seemed to be hoping I'd come around.

"You should be careful with her," Mike said.

"What do you mean?" Isaac asked.

"She's insane," Mike replied.

"Mike—" I started, but Isaac held up a hand to silence me.

"It's okay, dear, I've got this," Isaac said to me softly. He looked at Mike with anger. "Why would you say that, Mike?"

"She sees things," Mike said. "Hears things. Can't trust she'll be who she says she is one moment to the next."

"We all have our struggles," Isaac said dismissively.

Mike's face reddened. "You can't seriously be considering letting her into the Independents. She's crazy!"

"I don't need to justify myself to you," Isaac spat. "In fact, if I were you, I'd be much more worried about yourself."

"You can't be serious," Mike said. "You're defending *her*? Do you know how I found out about this mental disorder of hers? I found her on the floor, soaked through from the rain. She had no idea where she was or how long she'd been lying there."

"That's enough, Mike," Isaac said. "We're not here to expose everyone's private life. It's not becoming of someone from my circle, first of all. It's also just embarrassing for you. And you can't come into my home and insult my guests."

"You don't get it, she–" Mike said.

"I'm afraid *you're* the one who doesn't get it," Isaac said. "You're not welcome here anymore, Mike. Clear?"

"But–" Mike began.

Isaac shoved him, hard. Mike stumbled back.

"I said, are we clear?" Isaac asked.

"Clear, clear!" Mike exclaimed. He turned on his heels and left the mansion.

When Isaac turned around to look at me, his anger had vanished. In its place was a smile.

"There. That's better, isn't it?" he asked. "Now it's just you and me."

"Thank you," I said quietly.

"Is it true, what he said?" Isaac asked. "About finding you on the floor?"

"Yes," I said.

"And why were you on the floor?" Isaac leaned closer. I could smell his cologne, some smoky mix of pine and other earth tones.

"I lose track of things sometimes," I admitted.

"And do you lose yourself, too?" he asked, seeming concerned.

"Sometimes. I think I should get going. I'm pretty tired."

"I understand. It's been a rough night for you. But we'll talk about this more later, all right? Promise me."

"I promise," I said.

"Good," Isaac replied. "Now get home. My staff will make sure you get there safe and sound. And Kate? Don't forget to finish reading my book."

*

When I got home, all I could do was lie in bed and relive the confrontation with Mike. Jer lay beside me, his head resting lightly on the pillow.

"I don't know what to do," I said. "That gig was a mess."

"You didn't expect Mike to be there. You couldn't have known he was involved with Isaac's people."

"I just stood there and let him talk for me," I said. "Like he was my knight in shining armor or something."

"Is that how you see him?" Jer asked.

"No!" I exclaimed. "No. I don't. But I think he's a great guy. I just wish I had stood up for myself."

"I get it," Jer said. "But don't be too hard on yourself. A lot of things happened tonight that you didn't expect. That you couldn't have predicted."

"And," Veronica said from the doorway, "there were a few things you could have done better."

"I knew it was only a matter of time before you chimed in," I muttered.

"Don't wallow alone," Veronica said. "You do better when you have someone else around."

I decided to call Brielle over. She arrived within the hour.

"Oh, honey," Brielle said when I opened the door. "You've been through a lot."

She wrapped her arms around me. I sank into the comfort of her embrace.

"Tell me everything that happened," Brielle said as I closed the door behind her.

We got comfortable on the couch, and I told her everything, from wearing Isaac's wife's dress, to Mike's appearance at the gig.

"I can definitely see how Mike being there would upset things," Brielle said. "I'm sorry, Kate."

"Thanks, B," I said.

She took my hand and squeezed it. I squeezed back.

"I just hope you know Mike is wrong when he calls you insane," Brielle said. "You're not. You have issues, true, but you're coping with them great as far as I can tell. You're working on yourself. That's worth something."

"I appreciate you saying so," I told her.

"I've been so worried about you. I'm just glad you're doing okay after all of that happened at the gig."

"Thank you. I'm happy you're here. I really didn't want to be alone."

"You're welcome. I don't want you to be alone when you're distressed like this, either."

"I'm glad it's you who's keeping me company. I really need to be around someone safe. Someone I trust."

"And when you say you trust me, does that include your alters?" Brielle asked.

I smiled. "Yes. Them, too. We all trust you."

"I'm so glad. I was worried maybe they wouldn't like me."

"No way. Veronica and Jer are both fans."

"And you?" Brielle asked. "Are you a fan?"

"A big one," I replied.

Brielle moved closer to me on the couch. Only a couple of inches separated us now. "I'm a big fan of yours, too."

I blushed. "You've always been one of my biggest supporters."

"And I admit that part of that is because of how I feel about you," she said. "You should know that as soon as I walked in here tonight, I wanted to kiss you."

"Oh," I breathed. Veronica's elation bubbled up from my chest. "Really?"

"Yes." Brielle slipped a hand across my cheek. "I still really want to. Would you be okay with that?"

"Yes."

She kissed me softly, tenderly. I sank into her touch. Hugging her had felt so safe and comforting. Kissing was even better than that. I felt like nothing could hurt me, not Mike, nothing. And

Veronica's happiness shone through. A smile appeared on my lips.

"I'm glad I make you happy," Brielle said as she pulled back, noticing my smile.

"You make all of me happy," I said. "I never realized what was missing from my relationship with Mike. But a big part of it was that not all of me liked him, only a small fraction of me did. But now that I've kissed someone all my alters are on board with, I have to say it's a far better experience."

Brielle laughed. The sound warmed me. "That's great! You know, I intend to care for all of you. Not just the pieces I like. I love you for who you are. That means all of you."

I paused for a moment, startled by how easily she had told me she loved me. But we had said it so many times before, as platonic friends. Now, it held a different meaning. But it didn't scare me. It brought me comfort. I knew she meant she cared about me.

*

Isaac had been blowing up my phone with requests for songs and ideas for future gigs. Or, I should say, Hilda had been messaging me on his behalf. Still, it seemed like despite how things went at his reading, he was willing to hire me to play for him again. The stuff with Mike hadn't phased him. In fact, he seemed more interested now than ever. I was flattered by the attention. It felt nice to have someone appreciate my music, even if Veronica was wary about him. I thought he was strange, but nice. And supportive, too. That won him extra points.

I was grocery shopping when I saw him next. He seemed entirely out of place in a grocery store. For some reason, I assumed he would have had someone on staff to shop for him. But there he was, in white jeans and a plain white T-shirt, with a basket in his hands. We were both standing next to the fruit section near the entrance to the store.

"Kate!" Isaac said when he saw me. "What are the chances?"

"I was thinking the same thing," I said as he drew me into a hug. I hugged him back. "I didn't think you would do your own shopping."

"It's relaxing, believe it or not, if you avoid the rush. Don't you think?"

"It can be. Wandering between aisles, when there's nobody else around. Sure, it can be relaxing."

"I hope I haven't been overwhelming you with notes since your performance," Isaac said. "I just can't stop thinking about how well you played, and how excited I am for the next time."

"Thank you," I said.

"And you know, I've been thinking about the things Mike said, too."

"Oh really?" I asked. "Like what?"

"He mentioned you hear things. See things, sometimes." Isaac gestured vaguely in the air. "I'd love to know more about that."

"I wish Mike hadn't mentioned it..."

"Don't be embarrassed!" Isaac smiled. "We're just two people, talking. There's nothing to be ashamed of. You have a condition. I just want to learn more about it."

"I'm not sure the grocery store is the best place to talk about it."

"Then let's go for a drive," he suggested.

I looked at my basket. I had a few bananas, some apples, and a handful of granola bars.

"I don't have anything that needs to be refrigerated," I said. "I can throw them in my backpack like I was planning."

"Yeah?" Isaac beamed. "You wouldn't mind?"

"No," I said. "Let's do it."

I bought my things. Isaac bought his. He had an equally unimpressive haul. Two sodas, some baby carrots, and a box of crackers. I had only gone in to pick up some snacks, and it seemed like he had been there for the same reason.

I followed him out into the parking lot. He led me to his car. A shiny, brand-new BMW. I felt very small when I sat in the passenger seat. The car was massive. He smiled at me as he buckled himself in.

"I hope you don't mind all my questions," he said. "I just find you so fascinating."

"Thank you." Heat rose to my cheeks. It was nice to not only have my music appreciated, but to be appreciated for who I was, too. Isaac didn't shy away from my mental illness the way that Mike had.

"So, tell me, what kinds of things do you see and hear?" Isaac asked as he pulled out of the parking lot.

"I see people," I said. "Usually the same ones. It's a bit complicated, but these people are a part of me."

"Part of you how?"

"I see the world through their eyes sometimes. I get a lot of feedback on life from them."

"Sounds useful," he said. We were on the road now, heading toward the highway. "Like having a devil on one shoulder and an angel on the other. Always there to give you advice."

"Something like that," I said, amused at the thought of Veronica as a devil and Jer as an angel. It suited them.

"What did they think of me? Of the reading the other night?" Isaac asked. "Since these people you see seem to be advisors of sorts. I want to hear what they had to say."

I hesitated. I didn't want to tell him what Veronica thought, because she was critical of him. I decided to go with Jer's opinion instead.

"Most of it went over my head," I said. "I haven't read enough of your book yet to get a sense of the impact. But Jer...that is, one of the people I see, he's in support of me working for you."

"I'm glad to hear that. So, one of the people you see is a man?"

"Yeah."

"And what's he like?" Isaac asked.

"He's gentle, kind, and calm."

"Sounds like a nice guy to have around," Isaac remarked.

"He is, yeah," I said.

"Do you consider these people to be real, like you and me?"

"They're real in their own way. But I also know that they're not really here. Not in the same way you and I are."

"Interesting. And you respect them like real people," Isaac said.

"You could say that, yeah," I replied.

"So, what they want matters? What they dream about? If they even have dreams."

"One of them does. One of them wants me to rise in the ranks and become a musical success."

"Stick with me, kid, and your dream might be a reality," Isaac said with a smile.

I smiled back. "Thank you. I really appreciate how you believe in me and my music. And I also appreciate how you defended me against Mike the other day. It wasn't necessary, but I'm still thankful you were there to stand up for me."

"No worries. Mike's vibes were all wrong, in the end. But yours, I like. A lot."

"You keep mentioning vibes," I pointed out. "I don't

remember reading about those in your book."

"It's less a book thing and more an in-person thing," Isaac replied. "I like to evaluate each person I let into the group, to see if their vibes match mine. Usually I'm pretty spot-on with folks, but occasionally I'll slip up, like I did with Mike."

"I had no idea he was part of your group at all."

"Yep, he's been an Independent for a few months now."

I recognized the word Independent as the name they chose for themselves.

"You know, it's interesting that you think my vibes are good," I said. "Because Mike definitely didn't."

"He doesn't know what he's talking about," Isaac said. "You're interesting, Kate. And that's far more valuable than whatever Mike could bring to the table."

"What did you see in him?" I asked.

"What did you?" Isaac shot back.

"Fair enough." I let out a little laugh. "I guess I thought he was the kind of guy you could always rely on. He was usually there for me when I needed him. Usually. But more and more I started to realize there were things about him I didn't like."

"And this was, I suppose, thanks to these people you see?"

"I call them alters, but yes. In part, it was due to them."

"So, they play a big role in determining who you keep around in your life," Isaac remarked.

"Yeah, I suppose they do."

"Other than Mike showing up for you occasionally, what else redeemed him?"

"He was kind, I thought. Soft-spoken, most of the time. And he prided himself on being independent. I guess it makes sense why he was drawn to your group."

"We put a lot of emphasis on finding yourself from within,

not from outside," Isaac said. "That interested Mike a lot."

"And yet when it came to me, he wanted me to stay quiet about it, rather than talk about possible options or even explore therapy."

"You went to therapy together?"

I nodded. "It didn't go too well, though. He showed up. That's about all I can say."

"Sounds like a nickname is starting to form. The Show-Up Guy."

I laughed. "That's not a bad nickname, actually."

Isaac glanced at me sympathetically. "I can see how that would leave a lot to be desired."

"It wasn't the best relationship."

"And how are things looking now for you, romance-wise?" Isaac asked.

I felt we were really bonding over discussing my alters and how they affected me, but my love life was territory I was a bit more hesitant to get into with him, especially since things with Brielle were so new. But I trusted him, and he seemed like a harmless type.

"I've been interested in one of my best friends," I admitted. "It's been a long time coming. We've known each other since high school, but I never realized I had romantic feelings until recently."

"Wow, since high school." Isaac whistled low. "That's a long time."

"But enough about that." I was keen to move the conversation to a less intimate topic. "Tell me more about why you let Mike become an Independent."

"It's kind of like you said: he showed up. He came to every meeting, he read the book, and seemed to devote himself to our way of life. About finding light from within."

"I wonder if his troubles with me had anything to do with how passionate he was about becoming an Independent."

"It's possible," Isaac replied.

"He seemed to think that I wasn't healing properly. Because I was relying too much on other people, and not enough on myself."

"Did *he* tell you that?"

"No, it's what I figured out after everything he said. He wanted me to take medication and just silence these voices in my head."

"I'm glad you didn't," Isaac said. "It sounds like they've been a great help in guiding you." He motioned to the road. "Would you like me to drop you off at your place?"

"Sure," I said. I didn't need to give him directions. He punched my address into his car's navigation system and it showed him the route there.

"Thanks for the talk," he said. "I really appreciate learning more about you."

"Thanks for listening," I said. "And for the opportunity to work with you. I've been really hoping to find a regular gig, and this is just what I needed."

"I'm glad." He seemed to mean it. "We've been wanting live music at our events for a while, but it's been hard finding the right person. You fit the bill, though. Speaking of which, I'll have Hilda send over your earnings from last time."

"Thank you."

"And I'm doing another reading this Tuesday. I'd love it if you could attend."

"I'll be there," I said. "For sure."

We rode the rest of the way in silence. It felt comfortable, despite not knowing much about him. He had a certain way about him that radiated confidence and assured you that you had nothing to worry about.

*

Dinners with Brielle were always enjoyable, and a big part of that was due to her excellent cooking. She always prepared the best dishes. Tonight, she had chosen a favorite of mine, rice pilaf. She made it with aged parmesan, which I loved. We sat on the couch as we dug into our fancy food. We didn't exactly thrive on etiquette.

"Thank you for making all of this," I said. "It tastes so good!"

"You're welcome," she said. "I'm glad it's to your liking."

I told her about how I had run into Isaac at the grocery store, and how we had gone for a drive. "He seems really into learning more about my condition. Bri, I can't believe I landed a gig this good with a boss this compassionate!"

"That's amazing," Brielle said. "I'm really happy for you. And you're right, it *is* an amazing gig. Think of the opportunities this could lead to. Plus, you're making a pretty penny for your music. That's gotta feel good."

"It does. It feels really good."

"You did well. And Isaac likes you."

"Yeah. He invited me to attend his next reading. I'll probably be playing more of the same, unless I can write something new before Tuesday."

"What kinds of questions did he ask you?" Brielle asked.

"He was mostly curious about my alters. If they had dreams and aspirations of their own. How much I listened to their advice."

"And was he of the same opinion as Mike? That you should just take medication and make it all go away?"

"No, he said he was glad that I decided to do therapy instead.

He says he finds it all really fascinating."

"I've noticed something," Brielle said. "He knows a lot about you, but can you say the same about him? How much do you know about him?"

"Not much," I said. "Why?"

"Because trust is a two-way street. And I can tell he's really winning you over. But I think it's always good to be cautious in these situations."

"What are you saying?" I asked.

"I'm just saying that maybe we should do a little research on this guy. Level the playing field a little bit."

"Research? Like what?"

"Well, for starters, have you even googled him?" Brielle asked.

I shook my head. "Nope."

Brielle set her empty bowl on the side table. "All right. Let's do that now." She pulled her phone out of her pocket and punched in Isaac's full name, Isaac Reynolds. I peeked over her shoulder. Loads of ads showed up for his book. But that wasn't the only interesting element. There were also articles about the Independents. Brielle clicked on the Wiki.

"It says here there's a section on controversy," Brielle said. "Should we read it?"

"Of course," I said. "Skip to the juicy bit."

"In 2020, the group was accused of being a cult," she read. "These rumors were staunchly denied by Mr. Reynolds. However, when interviewed, a group of anonymous former Independents reported that Isaac ran his business and religious group like a cult."

"I wonder what that means," I said.

"I don't know," Brielle replied. "It's all pretty vague here. I wonder if these people just had grudges against Isaac and wanted to ruin his name."

"Seems like it," I said. "All he does is read to a group of people from philosophy books that he wrote. He really isn't doing anything nefarious at all that would warrant calling it a cult. Is there any more information on Isaac on there?"

"It looks like he has a Wiki page of his own. It's pretty short, though."

"Let's see it."

She clicked her way through to his page. She scrolled down to the section on his personal life.

"It says here that he was married, but that his wife tragically passed away in a car crash," she said. "Together they had one child."

"Oh wow, so he's a father," I said. I tried to imagine him with a kid. He was so upbeat and friendly. It was easy to imagine him being a good father.

"*His* father was an actor. That's likely where all the money comes from, other than his own work."

"Famous?" I asked.

"Relatively," she said. "He's been in a few older movies that we've probably seen."

"I wonder what his parents think of his group."

"I wonder if they're part of it."

"Could be, given how much of a reach the Independents have. And having a famous actor as part of their crew would certainly give some appeal."

"You're right."

"Thanks for looking him up with me," I said. "I wouldn't have thought to do it without you. I don't mistrust Isaac, but it's good to know a little bit more about him."

Brielle smiled. "You're welcome."

We spent the rest of the evening watching old TV shows like *Angel*. This was one of our favorites. A quote stuck out to me during the episode we were watching, *Epiphany*. "If nothing we do matters, then all that matters is what we do," said Angel, the main character of the show. I thought those words held a lot more weight than anything Isaac had written in his book. If what I had read in Isaac's book was right, and the creator of the universe really did not care about what happened to us, then all that mattered was how we behaved in the here and now and that we knew ourselves for who we truly were. And I felt like with therapy, and now my work, I was on the right path to finding that out for myself.

Chapter Eight

November 2022

The second gig started off much the same as the first. At least two dozen people were milling about Isaac's gigantic living room, wearing ensembles composed entirely of white. I was set up next to the stage, with my violin case at my feet. I started off by playing a couple of originals that I had played last time. Although nobody stopped to listen, I caught a few people shooting pleased glances my way. They were enjoying the music.

When Isaac got on stage, he gave me a quick thumbs-up. I smiled at him. I was glad to be there, and I was glad to get his approval.

"Let's all put our hands together for our musician tonight, Kate!" Isaac said.

The crowd clapped politely. I bowed my head.

"Kate, why don't you come up here for a moment?" he said.

I hesitated. "Come on, it's all right!"

There were a few cheers from the crowd, encouraging me to do as he said. I walked up on stage. The lights were so bright, I could barely see the people standing in front of me. I felt disoriented and dizzy as my stage fright kicked in.

"Now, I've only recently met Kate. And, as some of you already know, she hasn't been initiated as an Independent. Yet." This got a few laughs from the audience. "But Kate is a talented musician, and I'm glad to have her with us here for the second Tuesday in a row. Give it up for our violinist!"

The crowd clapped louder this time. Once the applause died down, Isaac began his reading. Today's excerpt of his book had to do with how the universe was created. According to Isaac's book, there is a God, but this God is uncaring about justice. It is up to us humans to deal with such things. It was a fairly bleak outlook, but one he considered empowering, despite the cosmic indifference.

When the reading was done, Isaac motioned me over. I was hesitant to get back on stage, but I did as he asked.

"That was all very well done," I said. "Great reading."

"I can say the same to you," Isaac replied. "Great work tonight. The people loved you."

"I noticed you said I wasn't initiated yet. Do you have plans to invite me in?" I asked.

"I've been thinking about it. But I don't want to rush you into it. Have you finished the book?"

I had, indeed, finished it. Veronica had sneered almost the entire time I was reading it, but I powered through to the end. It largely seemed like a depressing take on positive thought and empowerment, but it was unique, and I liked that. Isaac had put his own spin on what had been done a hundred times over.

"Yes," I said. "Thank you for giving me the chance to read it.

And to attend these readings. I feel like I understand your philosophy better when I come to one of these events."

He grinned. "That makes me so happy to hear! That's why I have these events in the first place. To get people more involved. To help them understand my message."

"Well, you're doing great work. I really felt your reading resonated with me in ways that simply reading by myself couldn't."

"And I'm sure the relaxing ambiance you bring to the table didn't hurt, either." Isaac motioned to my violin.

"I'm glad you find my music relaxing," I told him.

"And inspiring," he said. "Our evenings really would not be the same without you."

I looked at the crowd. Despite not being able to see much, I could tell Jer was out there, watching me. Encouraging me. Letting me know I was safe, and everything would be okay. I tried to keep the image of him in my mind so that I wouldn't lose my nerve and dive off stage.

"You're fitting in quite well," Isaac said. "I think that's part of why I'd like to invite you to become an Independent."

"What's involved in the initiation?" I asked. I wondered if there was some kind of ceremonial rite of passage, or if I had to memorize his book.

It was neither.

"At this point, you just have to meet with my family," he said. "And if that goes well, and the vibes match up, then you're allowed in."

"Your family?" I repeated, at a loss for words. "Do you mean your parents, or...?"

"I mean my son, Max," he said. "He's very wise for someone his age. He's only five. But I feel that children can see right through some people. He's been a great judge of character so far, with Mike excluded from that list, of course. Everyone else has been wonderful."

I paused. So, he allowed a five-year-old to determine who he would let into his very exclusive group?

"I'll be happy to meet him," I said.

"He's a very old soul," Isaac said. "You'll see when you meet him."

"This guy can't be serious," Veronica muttered from my side. She had appeared wearing a white outfit, like mine, but didn't seem too pleased about it. She had her arms crossed and her shoulders slumped. "You're not seriously considering joining this group, are you?"

I ignored her. "What led you to allow Max to choose who gets in and who doesn't?"

"It all started when I had a reading here one night, and I let him attend. He was very reverent, as you can imagine. He hears a lot about Daddy's work but doesn't get to witness it in person very often. When he was here, people showed a different side of themselves. They were kinder, generally. But a few people treated him with disrespect. That got the immediate 'out' from me. I can't have people calling themselves Independents and treating my family with disrespect."

"How did they disrespect your family?" I asked.

"They said all sorts of things. Talked about how Max shouldn't be here, at a gathering for adults... That the topic was too tough for him to understand. Any Independent who thinks children should not be present gets the 'no' from me. Children have every right to learn about the Light from Within. Just as much as the adults."

I didn't pretend to understand the importance of this Light from Within, but I knew it was important to Isaac. It made sense to me that it would be important for him to impart all this knowledge to his son, too. After all, this was like his religion.

"I get it," I said. "If I had a child, I wouldn't want people saying he should go home, either."

"Yeah." Isaac smiled. "We're on the same wavelength there. That's why I think you should meet him. You've already done the hard part: reading the book. Now you just have to meet a five-year-old who will definitely love the crap out of you."

"Yeah? How do you know?"

"Because I think you're amazing already. How could he not?"

*

I met Isaac at the preschool before pick-up time. I was there to meet Max, and to potentially finalize my introduction to the Independents. Isaac stood out front. He waved to me as I approached.

"He should be here any minute," Isaac said. "Say, I was wondering, when you meet with Max, wouldn't it be interesting to let an alter do the talking for you?"

I hadn't considered this. I also didn't know how to explain to Isaac that it wasn't as simple as telling an alter to take control—it had to happen naturally and doing that spontaneously could be difficult.

"I could try," was all I said.

A line of children emerged from the building, all of them with big smiles on their faces. They shouted things I couldn't hear and ran toward their parents. Most of the adults waited there with their arms outstretched. It was heart-warming. Mila's presence tugged at my consciousness. She yearned for days like these—days where we had felt safe, too, running toward our mother after school. We missed those days. That's when I decided that if any alter was to interact with Max, the best one would be Mila.

"There he is," Isaac said, as a child walked toward us.

Max was small, even for a child his age. He had short brown hair, and bright-green eyes. He wore a white T-shirt, like his father, but with the added touch of jean shorts. He held a T-Rex toy.

"Hey there, champ," Isaac said as Max approached. He gave him a big hug.

"Hi, Dad," Max said. "Who's this?"

"This is one of my new friends, Kate," he said. "Kate, this is Max."

I knelt so that I was at his level. "Hi, Max. Nice to meet you. Is that a dinosaur you've got there?"

"Yeah!" he said, his face instantly lighting up. "Do you like dinosaurs, too?"

"I love them!" I replied. "I love dragons the most, but dinosaurs are a close second, since they have so much in common."

"I like dragons, too!" he said. "And Godzilla!"

"Have you seen the movie?" I asked.

Max jumped up and down. "Yes! Daddy took me to see it."

Isaac pressed a finger to his lips conspiratorially. "He may have been a bit young for that one, but you won't tell anyone, now, will you?"

"Your secret is safe with me," I said to Max. "I'm glad you enjoyed the movie. Was it not scary at all?"

"There were some parts where I was scared," Max said. "But it was a good movie."

"I'm glad, then," I said.

"Would you like to play with me some time?"

"I'd love that. I have a Nintendo Switch. Do you have one?"

"Yes! At home."

"Maybe we can play a bit of that together, too," I suggested.

I looked at Isaac for the first time in a while. What I saw surprised me. His eyes had welled up with tears. He was about to cry. I looked away, quickly, as if it would erase what I had just seen. But the man was clearly very emotional about my conversation with his son, which to me had seemed harmless. We were only talking about dinosaurs and monsters, after all. But that seemed to be enough to jerk a few tears out of Isaac.

"All right, buddy, let's get you in the car," Isaac said, his voice thick.

Max either didn't notice, or didn't care, because he ran off toward his father's BMW.

"It's really nice, seeing him so excited like that," Isaac said. "It's been a tough few years, what with his mother passing and all."

"I can't imagine how hard that must be," I said, standing up. "I'm very sorry for your loss."

"Thank you. You know, he rarely talks to people about Godzilla. He must really like you."

"That's great. So does that mean I'm 'in'?"

"You've definitely passed with flying colors. If you want in, you're in."

I was glad to hear that. Being part of the Independents meant that I had also secured my spot as their live musician, permanently.

"And," Isaac said, "I was hoping you would be interested in more than just the Independents."

"What do you mean?" I asked.

"I was hoping you would be interested in *me*, too. I know you mentioned you had a high school sweetheart, and I'm sure that's all well and good. But think about it for a second. You and me, together, we'd be unstoppable. Your talent, and my ingenuity, we could create something beautiful."

I gaped. I hadn't expected that. Veronica appeared next to him, shaking her head.

"I knew this wouldn't go how you wanted," she said.

"I'm sorry, but if you're suggesting we have some kind of relationship, I…" My eyes darted nervously to the parents surrounding us. I didn't want to have to reject him in front of the school, but he was leaving me little choice in the matter. "I can't do that."

"Why not?" Isaac's face fell. "Don't you think that we'd make a good team?"

"Is that why you wanted to initiate me?" I motioned to the school. "And why you had me meet Max? Because you wanted to date me?"

Isaac scoffed. "You're reducing it quite a bit."

"I think I'm seeing things clearly for the first time," Veronica said through me. "And I'm not liking what I see."

"Kate, wait a minute—"

"No." I stepped away from him. "I'm not doing this. Not here. Not in front of all these people. God, how stupid can I be?"

"You're not stupid," Jer said, from beside me. "You just got a bit lost."

"I genuinely thought you were interested in my work," I said. "But I'm just another prospect for you, aren't I?"

"There aren't many women out there like you," Isaac said. "I can guarantee you that. You're one of a kind, Kate. I didn't want to let you slip through my fingers."

I groaned internally. Every time he spoke, he seemed to make it all worse.

"I'm leaving now," I announced. "Do not follow me."

I felt secure in the knowledge that he would do as I asked, given that Max was in the car waiting for him. Still, I made sure to check over my shoulder every few minutes during the long walk home to check for any BMWs following me.

*

I sent back Isaac's dress the next day. My note was written as direct as possible, holding nothing back about what I really felt.

> *Isaac. I'm writing this to let you know I can't work for you again. This book was one of the worst, most nonsensical things I've ever read. It's completely anti-science and borrows from various different religions and mythologies while claiming to be original. I'm also not at all interested in you romantically. Your advances are not welcome. Please never invite me to another one of your gigs again.*

I hoped that had been clear enough. But to my dismay, I got a call from Hilda a few hours later.

"Hi, Kate?" Her voice was shaky.

"Hi, Hilda, it's me," I said. "What's up?"

"I got the note you sent," she said. "I thought maybe I'd offer to meet up to hear about your frustrations. Because it's pretty clear from your note how frustrated you are."

"I don't know…" I really wanted to stay as far away from anyone who knew Isaac as possible.

"Just for a coffee, please?" Hilda sounded anxious. I had a sense that her job might partly rely on getting me to be compliant. I didn't want her to get punished because of the note that I sent.

I let out a long breath. "All right. Let's have coffee."

"Great!" she said. "I'll be by with our car to pick you up soon."

Before I could protest, she hung up the phone. Within twenty minutes, Isaac's car was parked outside. I checked from my window. It was only the driver in the front, and Hilda sitting in the back. The rest of the car was empty. I was relieved. I went down to meet her.

She greeted me warmly as I got into the car. She wore a green dress today with a gold belt. Not white. I noticed she held the note that I had sent with the dress.

"You haven't passed that on to Isaac?" I asked.

"I thought it would be best if you and I spoke before I handed it over," she said. She looked at the driver, then shook her head. It didn't seem like she wanted to talk in front of him.

We spent the rest of the ride to the coffee shop in an awkward silence. Hilda appeared to be on the verge of tears. I felt bad for having put her in this situation but hoped I could clear things up with her once we got to the coffee shop. It was necessary for me to be that harsh with Isaac, so he would get the message.

The driver let us out in front of the coffee shop. I followed Hilda inside.

Once we sat down, Hilda leaned in to whisper to me. She motioned to the note. "I don't think I can give this to Isaac."

"Because it will upset him?" I asked. "I know that. It's why I wrote it the way I did. To upset him."

"But why would you do that?" Hilda asked, horror written plainly on her face. "You really don't want to upset Isaac."

"But I do," I argued. "I want him to know that I want nothing to do with your group. That I didn't enjoy his book. And that I won't be working for him again."

Hilda bit her lip. "Maybe we could find a way to reword it."

"I don't think so," I said.

"Why are you so upset with him?" Hilda asked. "You don't have to be rude here, Kate. You could be courteous."

"Because..." I stopped myself. I didn't have to justify myself to her. As much as I felt sympathy for her, I also had my own frustrations against her. "I don't know if it's even worth explaining it to you. I mean, you knew about the dress, didn't you? How could you let him give it to me? It was creepy, even you have to admit that."

"Isaac is a sensitive man. He's sentimental. He wanted to give you a piece of clothing he felt mattered. So, he chose something of Celine's, his wife."

"And you see no issue with this?"

"I can see why it would make you uneasy, but I promise you, he didn't mean to make you uncomfortable."

"Is that why you asked me to come here? So you can defend his actions?"

"No, no." Hilda sounded sincere. "I was just hoping we could find some way to relay your message without being so…harsh. I'm not here to tell you what to say or to stop you from speaking. I just think there must be a nicer way to put it all than to tell him his book is bad."

"But I didn't like his book." I could hear Veronica in my voice. She was near the front. I didn't try to stop her from taking control. "In fact, I thought it was bullshit. Aren't you glad I wasn't entirely honest? The note I wrote was tame in comparison to what I actually think. And I could have written way more. About how weird your whole cult is."

"Please, don't." I could see a sheen of sweat on Hilda's brow. "You really don't want to get on Isaac's bad side."

"Is that a threat?" I asked.

"No, it's a warning," Hilda said. "Life will be much better for you if you stay on his good side. Believe me."

I laughed in disbelief. "This is insane. I worked *two* gigs for him and now I have to placate him? He's not my boss anymore, Hilda, he's yours."

"Yes, and I ask that you take some pity on me here. You have some idea of what he's like. I've worked with him for years. I can tell you right now that if I hand him this note the way it is, it'll cause an explosion."

I crossed my arms in front of my chest. "I'm not rewriting it. You can give it to him as is. I'll deal with the fallout."

"It's really best if you reconsider," Hilda insisted. "I don't think you're ready to deal with Isaac when he's upset. He can be a bit...unreasonable."

I considered her pleading expression. She seemed genuinely distressed. It appeared my note would affect not only my relationship with Isaac, but his attitude toward his staff. His behavior was by no means my responsibility to control, but I also realized the power I held here over his mood. And Hilda seemed convinced I could save her a bit of grief by changing the note.

"What would *you* suggest I say?" I asked.

"I would suggest you simply tell him that you've found work elsewhere, and thank him for the opportunity," she said. "I'll take care of the rest. You don't need to mention not liking his book at all."

"Okay." I shrugged. "Fine. We'll leave the book out of it."

Hilda reached for her purse and pulled out a pen and notebook. "Perfect. I brought this so you could write a new one."

I scribbled down what she had suggested quickly, and added, *I don't think that your group is right for me. But I wish you success with all your future plans.* I had to stop myself from writing profanities. Veronica was screaming in my mind not to be polite, to tell Isaac off. I resisted.

Flat words. Insincere words. But placating words, nonetheless. Hilda said she would take care of the rest. If Isaac was as unstable as Hilda made him out to be, I hoped that these words would work at keeping him calm.

I handed her the note. She crumpled the old one and got up to throw it out. Before she could reach the garbage can, she froze in place. In walked a man dressed entirely in white. Isaac. He had followed us here, somehow. Probably tipped off by the driver who had brought us to the coffee shop. He had a stormy look in his eyes.

"What's this?" I heard him ask Hilda. He took the crumpled note from her hand, unfolded it, and read it. I watched as his face sank. Then his eyes darted up to meet mine. "You."

"Isaac," I started, standing up from my seat to rush to Hilda's side. "I wasn't expecting you to be here."

"And I didn't expect you to be so brazenly outspoken," Isaac said. "Yet here we are."

"Sir," Hilda said. "You have to understand, that note was a first draft. She wrote another one, one that you were meant to see. That one is..."

Isaac lifted a hand to silence her. He pocketed the note. "I don't need to see the other one. This one is perfectly fine."

"Sir?" Hilda asked nervously.

Isaac's face settled into a calm mask. Gone was the stormy look in his eyes. "I thank you for your honesty, Kate."

I blinked. "You're welcome."

"I don't often get really honest feedback these days." He looked pointedly at Hilda. "Most people are too afraid of upsetting me to tell me how they really feel." Isaac hooked his arm into mine and pulled me toward the door. "Walk with me."

He hadn't given me much of a choice, and Hilda shot me a sympathetic look as we walked out onto the street. Isaac's driver nodded at us as we passed by, confirming my suspicions that he had tipped his boss off as to where we were.

I was uncomfortable with his arm hooked into mine, but he had a firm grip on me, squeezing my arm. His pace was clipped. I struggled to keep up.

"So, you're not mad about the note?" I asked.

"Certainly not," he replied. "I'm glad that you felt you could be real with me. The most important thing, Kate, is that you can always be real with me."

"Then let me be real." I stopped walking and jerked my arm out of his grip. "I don't like it when you touch me without asking. I don't like how you behave around me. It's misogynistic."

Isaac laughed. "There's that fire I was talking about. Go on! Keep going."

I balled my fists at my side. "I don't like how you patronize me, either, but that's neither here nor there. I just need you to know, Isaac, that I can't be in your group. I can't play at your gigs anymore. Not now that I know what really goes on."

"I don't mean to patronize you, honey," Isaac said. "I'm trying to encourage your honesty. I love it. It's refreshing."

"Are you daft?" Veronica asked through me. "I said I don't want to work with you anymore. I don't know how much clearer I can be."

"You'll change your mind," Isaac said. "In time."

"No, I won't!" I exclaimed. "And nothing you can say will make me."

"Why, because of the dress?" Isaac asked. "I'll admit, I should have realized the honor of wearing Celine's clothes might have been a bit too much for you. It was your first gig, and I gave you something far too precious. I was overeager. But can you blame me when you're so magnificent?"

"Magnificent? You've got to be kidding me."

"I'm very serious," he said. "I have a vested interest in you,

Kate, for many reasons."

"And what reasons are those?" I wasn't sure I really wanted to know.

"You're complex. I've never met a woman like you. And that's saying nothing about your musical talent. You're incredible. And I've only just scratched the surface. After our little fight with Mike, I know there's so much more to you. And I want to learn it all."

"I'm sorry, but no," I said firmly. "I don't want to work for you again. And I definitely don't want to be involved with you. It's going to be a no."

"You don't know what you're missing," he said, stepping closer.

"I think I'll be fine." I backed away from him. "Please, respect my decision."

"Or what?" he asked, a glint in his eye. "You'll call the police on me?"

"If you don't leave me alone, I might have to." I wondered how I had ever found him charming.

"Please." He laughed. "We're having a simple conversation here. There are no threats being made. Well, not from me, anyway."

"Look, Isaac, I think your book sucked," I said. "I didn't like it at all. And all this forced positivity crap? It's exactly that. Crap. And your white outfits are tacky."

Isaac laughed. "I'm sorry you feel that way. You might come around eventually on the outfits, though."

"No!" I yelled. Passersby paused to look at us before continuing on their way. I lowered my voice. "No. I'm not going to 'come around.' I'm done with you, okay?"

"I understand that you need some space," Isaac said. "And I'm willing to give that to you."

"Not just space, I need you out of my life."

"But Kate, don't you understand that not everyone is as generous as me?"

"What do you mean by 'generous'?"

"That once your next employer finds out about your mental health condition, they might not be as accepting. I'm giving you an opportunity to play at my gigs, with the full understanding of what is going on with you."

"I wouldn't say you have a *full* understanding," I retorted. "You know bits and pieces."

"I spoke some more with Mike," Isaac said. "I got him to tell me more about you. He was very willing to do so. Respectfully, of course. I couldn't have him disrespecting you in front of me."

"And what did he say?" I asked.

"He told me that you have multiple personality disorder. Is that what they call it now?"

"I don't have a formal diagnosis yet," I said. "And it's called dissociative identity disorder."

"Well, he told me that you have that, and I wanted to let you know I would never discriminate against you because of it."

"Interviewing my ex to gain information on my mental health is a total invasion of my privacy and doesn't win you points at all."

"He told me that you were attending therapy under a different name," Isaac went on as if he hadn't heard me. "I find that endlessly fascinating. Veronica, is it?"

At the mention of Veronica's name, my blood turned ice cold. "Don't talk about her."

"But why not? She's part of you, isn't she? I'd love to meet her someday. Is that even something that can be done?"

"You're meeting her right now," Veronica said through me.

"And she's here to tell you that you're being a dick."

"Am I?" Isaac looked shocked. "You certainly don't talk like Kate. I can see the difference in your face, too. How fascinating."

"I'm not some lab experiment for you to toy with," I said. "My mental health isn't some case study. I'm a real person."

"Of course, I'm sorry if I've caused offense," Isaac said. "It's just that I find you so interesting. I want to know more. Are there other alters?"

"I'm not answering that," I said.

"Oh, come on," Isaac pleaded. "Do you know how motivational someone like you would be for my religion? You could tell people your story. Show them that power comes from within. Your story would be an inspiration for so many."

"I'm not letting you use me as some cash cow for your cult," I snapped.

"I wouldn't put it like that," Isaac said. "And for the record, my religion is *not* a cult."

"If it looks like a duck, and quacks like a duck…" I looked him in the eye, not backing down. "Then it's probably a duck. You're a cult leader, man."

"I wish you wouldn't call it that," he said.

"I appreciate you giving me the chance to work for you, but like I said in my note, I never want to do it again."

Isaac's eyes narrowed. "Noted. But Kate, you should really reconsider this decision. It's probably the worst one you'll ever make." He scoffed. "I'm seriously interested in you. All these things that your ex considers to be insanity? I consider it to be a higher way of being. And I want to learn all about it."

"You'll have to take an abnormal psychology class, then, because it's not going to be through me," I spat. I was surprised by the venom in my tone, but knew it was due to Veronica's presence.

I was thankful for her anger. I wouldn't have been able to tell him off myself.

"Fine, have it your way," Isaac muttered. "But you'll regret this."

He went back to his car.

I ran the four blocks back to my apartment building. I looked over my shoulder almost the entire way, terrified that Isaac would follow me home.

He didn't.

*

After everything that had happened recently, I decided it was necessary to have another session with Naomi.

"How have you been, Kate?" she asked as we sat down together in her living room.

"I've been better," I admitted. "Things have been wild lately."

I filled her in on the details about the gig, the dress, Isaac's creepy advances, Mike's appearance at the mansion, and the fallout after I handed Isaac the note and told him I couldn't work with him anymore. I also told her about Brielle and me having kissed.

She listened attentively and nodded along as I spoke. "That sounds like a lot to handle."

"It was," I said.

"And how are your alters feeling about it all?" Naomi asked.

"Veronica was rightfully upset, but I was able to use her anger to finally tell Isaac off."

"And did it feel good? To get angry at him?"

"Yes, it did."

"It will likely continue to feel good when you take action that all your pieces agree on. In that moment, every part of you wanted to tell Isaac off, and you listened to yourself. Great work."

"Thank you," I replied.

"And how are your alters feeling about your new relationship with Brielle?"

"It might be a bit too early to call it a relationship. We only just kissed."

"And said you love each other."

"She said she loved *me*," I said. "But yeah. We do love each other. I just don't know if it's romantic love yet."

"Sounds like whatever it is, it's off to a good start."

"Yeah," I agreed. "I'd say so."

"Do you feel that the confrontation with Isaac has left any unresolved feelings in you?" Naomi asked.

I paused and reflected on the encounter. There were no regrets—I had spoken my mind and spoken clearly. But a heavy feeling weighed on me still.

"The thing that bothers me..." I started, then corrected myself. "No, not me. Veronica. The thing that bothers Veronica the most is that I didn't do it better."

"What do you mean?" Naomi asked.

"I could have handled him better. Done it all more effectively." I snorted. "It's just better when I'm in the front."

I realized dimly that Veronica had taken control. I didn't fight it. Naomi had taught me that I would feel at my best when everyone had a say. That included letting Veronica speak her mind.

"Everything would always be better with me at the front," Veronica said through me. "Kate messes everything up. Who got her out of this cult mess? Me. Who got her into a relationship with the most wonderful woman we know? Also me. If it weren't for me, Kate wouldn't have any good things in her life at all."

"I don't know if that's necessarily fair," Naomi said. "As

much as I remind Kate that you're all pieces of a whole, I have to remind you of the same thing, Veronica. She helps you just as much as you help her."

"Pfft. I don't see how. She barely does anything. She's a coward most of the time."

"But she's shown up to therapy," Naomi countered. "She's been present far more now, wouldn't you agree? Taken steps to move her life in the right direction?"

"I'd say that there are a *few* improvements, but..." Veronica began, but Naomi interrupted her.

"I don't think the constant stream of criticism is necessary or helpful. Why don't you try an exercise in self-compassion, and try to understand why Kate is afraid so much of the time?"

"I don't need to do any of that, because I understand Kate perfectly!" Veronica exclaimed. "It's her who hasn't taken the time to really get to know me."

"And do you think it's fair you have so much time up front these days, while Jer gets pushed to the sidelines?"

"I..." Veronica paused. "I didn't really think of that."

"No, I suppose you didn't," Naomi said. "But maybe try thinking of it now. Why doesn't Jer ever come to the front the way you do?"

"Because he doesn't have as much ambition as me," Veronica replied. "Because he doesn't know what's best. He's a bit of a doormat. He lets Kate walk all over him."

"Are you sure that's how you would describe him? Is that the kindest way you can put it?" Naomi asked.

"Maybe not the kindest way, but the most accurate," Veronica snapped.

"Veronica, I need you to really think here. You mentioned your relationship with Brielle being your success. That Kate had very little to do with it. But think on this for a moment. Would your relationship with her really work if it was just you? Or does Kate's softness have a certain appeal for Brielle?"

"I guess Bri does like Kate's softer side…" Veronica replied begrudgingly.

"Then you know you couldn't have gotten the relationship all on your own," she said. "And Brielle probably appreciates Jer's good cheer, too."

"And Mila," Veronica said. "Her playful and silly attitude shines through sometimes."

"Exactly," Naomi said. "You're all pieces of a whole that need to work together to accomplish things. And you do.

My senses calmed down. My body relaxed. Veronica had left the front.

"I'm back," I said. "It's Kate again."

"Hi, Kate," Naomi said. "Do you feel any better after letting all that out?"

"I do feel a bit better. Though mostly I'm a little dizzy."

"Don't worry, we'll take it slow from here. I'm really glad Veronica was able to admit that she needs you, and the others, to make things work. It might not seem like much, but it's a step in the right direction."

The rest of our session was spent discussing how I could better communicate with myself, and a few more exercises in self-compassion. Naomi suggested I incorporate self-compassion into my journaling, since it was something I was doing more regularly.

"What are your plans for the rest of the day?" Naomi asked.

"I'm going to see Brielle, actually," I said with a smile.

Epilogue

November 2024

Two years had passed since I first realized I was dissociating. Things had improved slowly but surely. I had moved in with Brielle and came out to my mother. It had been rocky at first, but she had accepted me being bisexual. She had also accepted my mental health struggles.

"You mean to tell me that you black out and behave as another person?" Mom asked over the phone.

"Sometimes, yeah," I said.

"And how did that start?" she asked.

"When I was young," I said. "Because of the things that Dad put me through. My mind created people who would protect me."

Mom paused. Silence on the other end of the line. Then, after a few uncomfortable moments, she said, "I'm so sorry."

"It's not your fault," I assured her.

"I know, but if I had been a better protector, you wouldn't have needed to do this." She sounded tearful.

"What matters most is I'm comfortable with who I am."

Naomi, who I still saw on a regular basis, told me that was the most important thing. That I was comfortable with who I was.

"Did you get an official diagnosis from a psychiatrist?" Mom asked.

"I've been working with a therapist for the last few years. We don't feel an official diagnosis is necessary. Things are easier now that I've had the right kind of therapy."

It was easier to strike a balance between my personalities and feel more like I was whole. The blackouts happened far less often, if at all.

"I'm glad that things are getting better for you," Mom said. "Give Brielle my love. And know that I am so, so sorry for my part in all of this. I never meant for you to be hurt."

"I know, Mom. I love you, too."

*

Tonight, I was playing for a crowd of two hundred people. Brielle and I were lounging in our apartment before I had to go.

"You're going to do great," Brielle said, her legs draped over me.

I smiled. "Thanks, babe. I'm pretty nervous, though. My stomach is in knots."

She rubbed my belly lightly. "Do you need a hot water bottle for it?"

"No, thank you. But I appreciate how thoughtful you are."

"And how is everyone else feeling about the concert tonight?" Brielle asked.

I liked how she phrased it. "How is everyone feeling?" had become an often-spoken phrase in our household. She wouldn't just check in with Kate, but everyone in my system of alters.

"Veronica is certain we'll do well," I said. "We've practiced. A lot. Thanks to her strict schedule. Jer thinks we'll do great, too. He'll be sitting in the audience with you, so if I look out, I'll be able to see you both there supporting me. Mila is a bit scared, but that just encourages me to step up and be brave."

"You've come so far," Brielle said. "I'm so proud of you. A year ago, you would have had difficulty telling me how everyone is feeling. Now it's just routine."

"Yeah. I think it's good progress, too," I said.

"Do you think that Hilda will come to this concert?" Brielle asked.

Hilda had been showing up to every one of my gigs for the last two years. She had only recently stopped. I should have known it wouldn't be that easy to get rid of Isaac and his Independents. She had approached me a few times, but after I told her off and threatened a restraining order, she backed off somewhat. But that didn't stop her from attending my shows and filming them. Sending the footage back to Isaac, presumably.

But for the last four gigs, she hadn't shown up. It seemed he had finally given up. It probably helped that the venues I was playing at were far nicer now and had decent security. Paying for tickets wouldn't have been an issue for Isaac, but a few words to security about the people dressed all in white, and they were quick to leave me alone.

"I ripped down a few posters for their cult," Brielle said, "when I saw some downtown the other day."

"Your service to society is appreciated," I said teasingly.

She took my hand in hers. "I'm glad they're finally learning to leave you alone. You were so brave, going up on stage every time like that, knowing she would be there in the audience and performing anyway."

"If I didn't perform, Veronica wouldn't let me live it down."

"And Mike?" Brielle asked. "Has he tried to get in touch at all?"

Even though it had been nearly two years since we had seen each other, Mike still texted me occasionally. It was likely when he was drunk and reminiscing over the past. He left me voicemails, too, which I always deleted. The few I had listened to were him asking for me to come back, saying he missed me.

"I've blocked his number," I said. "He'll probably keep calling and leaving voicemails from some other number, but it's been quiet on that end, too."

"So, tonight is all about you. A time for you to shine, all on your own."

"Tonight is about me and you," I told her. I kissed her. "If it weren't for you, I wouldn't be able to get up there and play."

"Give yourself more credit. Without Veronica, Jer, and Mila, you wouldn't be able to do it, either."

"You're right." I smiled. "Especially Veronica."

"Especially her," Brielle said with a smile. "Miss Drill Sergeant on the piano drills."

"If it weren't for my piano drills, you wouldn't be playing at a prestigious venue," Veronica said from the other couch.

"And for that I'm thankful," I said.

Brielle listened intently. She was accustomed to me speaking to myself. It was part of our day-to-day life. She never judged me for it.

"Just remember this, you're not alone," Jer said. "If you ever feel nervous up there, remember that we're all here for you."

"Even me!" Mila said from where she sat cross-legged on the ground.

"Thank you, everyone," I said. "I used to feel forgotten. Like nobody knew I was there. But now I feel more seen than ever. I feel respected. I feel like we can all work together. And I hope that continues."

"Of course it will," Jer said. "We're all here for you."

"Even you, Veronica?" I asked.

"Of course," she said flatly. "Do you even need to ask that?"

"Apparently not," I said.

Brielle stroked my hair. "Good talks?"

"Good talks," I confirmed.

"Everyone is ready for tonight?"

"Ready as ever. And I think I'm ready to let the audience see the real me."

"That's great, babe."

"I think I'll give a little speech before I play," I said. "Tell them what it's taken for me to get here. Get real, and personal. Share my story. About figuring out dissociation, about how it started when I was young. About the abuse I faced. The grooming at the hands of the cult. The struggles with therapy. And finding myself as a queer woman. I think it's a story that deserves to be heard."

Brielle gave me a soft kiss. "I couldn't agree more."

Acknowledgements

Thank you very much to my editor, Elizabeth Coldwell, and to the rest of the crew at NineStar Press who made this novel possible.

About the Author

Chelsi Robichaud writes and resides in Nova Scotia, Canada. She publishes sapphic romance and fantasy novels. She has also self-published two comics.

Email
chelsiwriter@gmail.com

Other NineStar books by this author

Bi-Furious

CONNECT WITH NineStar Press

Website: NineStarPress.com

Facebook: NineStarPress

X: @ninestarpress

Instagram: NineStarPress

BlueSky: NineStarPress

Threads: @ninestarpress